YOU
ARE
INTUITIVE

TRUST YOUR TRUTH
TAKE BACK YOUR POWER

NATALIE MILES
HOST OF *SO YOU THINK YOU'RE INTUITIVE*

Cover art and interior design by chriswilliamsdesign.co.uk.

Author photograph: Beth Crockatt.

ISBN: 978-1-7354710-1-3

www.natalie-miles.com
www.the-numinous.com

For my Spirit Team.

∞

There are many labels to describe the mystical, "higher power" energy we are working with when we connect to our intuition. Through the ages, people have labelled it Spirit, the Universe, God, Source, the big G in the sky, the Cosmos, angels, universal consciousness, life force, universal energy, your higher Self ... and many other human words that attempt to describe this numinous energy. One of my family's many labels for it is "Diddleydop" ... so anything goes!

Since it is not my job to tell you how you should identify with this deeply personal connection, you will see this symbol ∞ through-out this book any time I am referring to this energy, so that you can go ahead and insert whatever word works for you. And if you don't have one yet, see what lands for you along the way.

CONTENTS

Access the Intuitive Action Guided Meditations in this book via the online portal at:

www.youareintuitive.com

Or download the INTUITIVE COMMUNITY app on your Apple or Android device.

INTRODUCTION
YOUR INTUITION LED YOU HERE

Yes, you are intuitive. Yes, you were born with this gift. Just like every single human on this planet, this means you have the power to always make the right choices for you and to know that you are on the right path, no matter what. But if you're reading this book, chances are you've forgotten how to trust, connect to, and work with your own inner guidance system.

If you feel like this doesn't apply to you (the gift part, let alone the forgetting how to work with it part), you are also not alone. Perhaps you feel some fear or anxiety come up when you think about intuition. This is very common, as many of us have been shamed or made to feel uncomfortable about our gifts. Maybe you even feel like you need to hide this book away from your family and friends, or feel shy about reading it in public, as you're afraid of being branded a weirdo. Or perhaps you're wondering why you even picked it up at all, as this isn't normally "your kind of thing."

And yet you felt the call. And now here we are.

Know that whatever spark of curiosity or deeper impulse led you here, you are being called back to your truth. Part of you knows it's time to reestablish a deeper connection with yourself and the world around you. To feel more grounded and supported. To find the courage to heal what hurts, and to discover what's really blocking you from living the life you know is meant for you. And the same part of you knows that the way to access all of this is to take back your intuitive power.

But before we get going, let's talk about any expectations you might have about this book. The number one thing to remember is that you don't need "special powers" to connect to your intuition. This isn't a skill that's reserved for a select group of spiritual superstars, or an elite, privileged secret society. It's for everyone. It's for you. And while we're at it, let's dismiss any preconceptions you may have about what an "intuitive" looks like. It's time to scrap the stereotype of a fortune teller sitting in front of a crystal ball, promising to reveal your future. Intuitive people look like you and literally every person you pass on the street. We are your friends, your family, and your colleagues, simply going about our everyday lives. As for the "telling the future" stuff? Yes, it's possible to a degree once you connect to your intuition. But this goes so much deeper than knowing who you'll date next and when you'll land the job of your dreams. It's about reactivating a connection to who you really are, and accessing your inner knowing. Which sounds more like why you're really here, right?

WHAT IS INTUITION?

Simply put, your intuition is your own inner source of guidance, knowing, truth, and power. Being connected to your intuitive gifts also means living in alignment with the world around you, and noticing the signs, messages and directions constantly guiding you on. This work doesn't live on some out-there, ethereal plane. It doesn't require a secret map or special language. It's work you can do in the here and now, all day, every day, using the most mystical instrument of all: your body. Not that anyone gets taught this in school. We mainly think of our body as the physical vehicle that gets us from A to B. But it is actually your very own extra sensory intuitive time and space machine that's here to help you make choices that are in alignment for you, get inspiration, alert you to any red flags, and be a portal to connect to ∞.

You may receive intuitive guidance through feelings or deep knowings, or by hearing, seeing, smelling and even tasting "messages" about the next right action to take. On our exploration together, you're going to discover exactly how this guidance shows up in your own body and how to decode what these messages mean for you. The beauty being that each and every one of us connects to our gifts in a very personal way. Intuition is not a one size fits all skill. This book is here to teach you how to access your own unique abilities—or rather, *remind* you how to use them.

So by now you're probably asking: if this is such an awesome skill, and one that can help guide me and every other being on the planet to living the lives of our dreams, how did we "forget" how to use it? The answer to this question lies in a shared history of fear, oppression, and pain.

In the past our ancestors worked with their gifts as part of everyday life. Intuitively following the lunar cycles to produce the best crops. Travelling across the globe with no GPS, using nothing but their inner compass and the stars above for guidance. Determining which plants and trees could be used for healing and medicinal purposes. It was customary for kings, queens and the general population to sit with the local medicine person, elder or priestess, to ask for their help in connecting to their own intuition during times of sickness, famine, and war, or simply for answers to everyday questions about life. But over the millennia, intuition has been forced into hiding, laden with stigma, and shrouded with shame and distrust.

Advancements in agriculture in the Middle Ages led to the advent of the patriarchy, and the formation of systems for living that relied on a hierarchical power structure. This meant some people held the power of the material world (money and natural resources) while others worked in service of those who controlled these resources. Those in charge were therefore threatened by people connecting to their own *inner power*. They didn't want people "below them" creating *power struggles* and challenging the status quo.

"Power" is a word you will read a lot in this book. Power is my word for the part of our life force energy that gives us agency to act on our free will, and just like intuition, we all have access to it. But because of the way power is often abused, we sometimes think of it in the negative. But when in balance, being in our power means being giving, flexible, supportive, and in flow. On the flipside, where use of power energy becomes controlling and authoritarian, it manipulates and appropriates. People can become addicted to power (which also materializes in the energy of money) and will try to hoard it and keep hold of it by whatever means possible. We only need to look at what's currently happening on our planet to see this in action.

As we've already touched on, when we are in our own intuitive power we are a force to be reckoned with. Power works hand-in-hand with intuition to enable us to act on our authentic truths, and live in alignment with who we really are. It has the energetic force of actionable change. So you can see why, throughout history, and even to this day, those hoarding the power also want to control access to our intuitive gifts. When we are connected to our intuition, it's like we are plugged directly into our own *inner* source of power—versus being beholden to the power structure that governs over us.

So in this new patriarchal establishment, the power was typically held and controlled by a select few, and they made it so that women (females and female identifying individuals) had to be obedient and dependent on them. To make this a reality and gain control, they required women to forget, mistrust or hide their "feminine" intuitive spiritual beliefs and practices. In the case of the white colonization and slave trade of the Americas, Africa, Asia and Oceania, *all* people outside of the dominant power structure were forced to submit to the dominant power structure and give their personal power away. To ensure that people stayed submissive and disconnected from their gifts, there followed a global campaign to brand intuitive practice as the "devil's work," instilling fear and mass hysteria about any communication with ∞ outside of organized religion. In Europe and across colonial North America between the 14th and 17th centuries, the practice of any form of intuitive craft was outlawed. Although there's no exact number on record, it's thought that tens of thousands, perhaps even millions, lost their lives in the "witch trials" that bred a climate of fear during this era.

Targeting mainly lower class women (although masculine identifying people were killed too), punishment included being tortured or death by hanging, drowning, or being burnt. These were the healers, herbalists, midwives and other forms of intuitives. And while this all took place centuries ago, anybody descended from this lineage is still holding onto the ancestral fear and pain of these traumas. Passed from generation to generation, this alone could be enough to block a person from feeling safe to embrace the gifts they were born with; the *power* that is their birthright.

This book is also an opportunity to begin to heal this shame. And in doing so, to prevent the stigma about intuition from being passed on to *your* descendants, keeping future generations separated from *their* power. Imagine a world where it is encouraged for us to *trust our inner knowing,* instead of fearing it. A place where people are free to connect to their own sovereign energy, and see intuition as an integral human and spiritual technology. I see this as a vital missing piece in us forging a stronger connection between ourselves, our planet, and the global collective energy. And it begins with each of us acknowledging, healing and taking back our own intuitive gifts TODAY.

∞∞∞

So who am I to be telling you all this?

First and foremost, I'm writing this book because *I am you.* Meaning, I've been exactly where you are now. Everything you'll find in this book is what I wish I'd known when I first started to connect to my intuition. When I was looking for support, all the information out there was super "woo-woo" and had a New Age vibe I found unrelatable, stale, and clichéd. I didn't vibe with any of the people teaching on the topic as I didn't see myself in them. I wanted straight forward, real-world advice that made connecting to my intuition seem as "normal" as brushing my teeth. This search led to me creating my podcast, *So You Think You're Intuitive?*, and eventually here, as it's become my personal mission to make this work accessible, engaging and grounded in the world we live in.

But when I first started to connect to my intuition it brought up doubts and fears for me, too. *Am I making all this up? Can I trust what I'm hearing? What if I see something scary? Do I even want to connect to this gift? Will I be able to turn it off?* But as I grew more confident, it began to feel like I was coming home to a part of myself that had been buried away for lifetimes, waiting to be reactivated. It made me feel powerful. It made me feel whole. And it also made me realize that I am never alone.

On this journey you will discover that you also have a "Spirit Team" to support you every day of your life. I like to think of them as my personal cheer squad. This team is made up of Spirit Guides, ancestors and deceased loved ones who are here to help guide you, protect you and send you messages. As part of this team we all have one main guide, which you can simply think of as a supportive spiritual energy that is with you from the moment you're born until you die. Chances are they have been our guide in multiple lifetimes, meaning during any past lives you have led before this one. They know you on a deep soul level, and if, for whatever reason, your tie has been severed, reconnecting with them is a very special experience—and one that I will guide you through in this book.

I had my first encounter with what I've come to know as my main Spirit Guide aged five (you'll hear the whole story later). But I didn't realize I was intuitive until age 16, when my mum took me to my first ever psychic circle—a gathering of women led by a local psychic in her home in a suburban village in the South of England.

I was so nervous, especially as I was the youngest there by at least 20 years, but I was made to feel welcome by the group. And it was on this evening that I really opened myself up to receive messages from ∞. During the guided meditation that opened the session, I felt an energy envelop me that I'd never experienced before; a feeling of floating and rising up, but at the same time being completely grounded and connected to my body.

It was that evening when I also gave my first ever "message" to someone. After being paired with a woman named Wendy, I was instructed to try it out to see if I could share any messages with her. I was nervous and didn't think I'd be able to do it, and I kind of felt bad for her that she'd been partnered with the rookie. When I shut my eyes all I could see was CAKE. Floating cakes of all different colors and sizes all around her. Then I saw her in a cake shop. I thought: *Am I making this up?* I opened my eyes, and with nervous anticipation I shared what I'd seen. She replied excitedly: "Oh yes I love making cakes. It's my favourite thing to do! It's my dream to one day open a cake shop." So what I saw *was real*! I could do this. The sensation that flooded my body was electric. I left the circle feeling inspired, more confident in myself, and as if I was seeing the world with a fresh pair of eyes.

Yes, Wendy went on to open her cake shop—but was this the start of me sharing my new found gift with the world? Hell no. This was when I began to *hide* my intuition, a pattern that stretched into my late teens, twenties and early thirties. I was so worried what friends, romantic partners and work colleagues would think of me. I didn't want to be labelled as weird, woo-woo, or downright crazy. I didn't want people to think I was making stuff up. It felt safer just to be Normal Nat. But my gifts didn't go away. I would occasionally "know things" about people without them telling me, or I'd feel the presence of loved ones who had passed. Sometimes I'd see other people's Guides walking down the street next to them, and I definitely made intuitive life choices based on "Hell Yes" feelings in my body that went against all logic. At home, my mum and I would sometimes share messages with each other, or mention if a deceased family member was around. Or we'd play spirit guide dominos, where you let your guide pick the domino for your turn instead of you. But during this period in my life I wasn't *consciously* choosing to call on my Guides or tuning into my intuition for answers. I guess you could say I was an *intuitive in hiding*.

Which worked fine ... until it didn't. In 2012, a series of rocky life changes led to my Spiritual Reactivation—a phenomenon we all experience, and which I discuss at length in Chapter 1. In fact, it could be your own "reactivation" that led you here, coupled with a feeling that something bigger is unfolding in your life. In which case, you've definitely come to the right place. Ultimately, it was my Reactivation that kick-started me taking back my intuitive power. I got the completely illogical knowing hit in my whole body to leave my job, my family, and my friends in London, and move to Vancouver, Canada. I'd visited on vacation a few years earlier and said to myself then, "one day I'm going to live in this city." It was here, without the safety net of my regular routine, and feeling lonely, lost and questioning what I was doing with my life, that I was divinely led to find another psychic circle where I could practice connecting with my gifts. Part of me knew that this would be the start of a deeper healing journey.

Vancouver became my city of death and rebirth. I began proactively connecting to my gifts by attending weekly psychic development circles. Now that I turned the tap back on, there was no going back. My mentor at the time said to me one day: "Nat you know you're going to do this full time, right?" I laughed and didn't believe her. I was still working at a production company, telling my colleagues I was going to "meditation circles" after work so they didn't judge me. But ∞ had other ideas and I was let go, my boss simply observing: "Nat you're not happy. Go and find what makes you happy." Which, in turn, began the journey to leaving film and starting up my own intuitive led business giving psychic readings for people.

Finally, I was beginning to not only trust but *embody my own truth*. By tuning in daily, I learned to trust my own inner guidance rather than relying on external sources. I had more confidence expressing myself. I experienced a new sense of direction and purpose. To my amazement, my life began to transform physically, energetically, and spiritually, and I was able to use my gifts to find love and create financial abundance for myself (more details on this part later, too!). I felt like I was tapping into an immense source of power that had always been flowing all around me, but which I was now inviting to play and express itself through me.

◇◇◇◇◇

Which all sounds great, doesn't it? And I want all of this for you, too. But this isn't just a book about how to connect to your intuition. It is also an invitation to reclaim your own Energetic Self-Sovereignty and take the steps to heal what hurts in your life.

As we move through the new millennium, spirituality has become a multi billion dollar industry, where the focus is often on inviting in "love and light" and "manifesting your dream life." Which can be very healing and lots of fun ... but is only half the picture when it comes to inviting intuition, or ∞, into your life. Language like this, and practices which focus on improving your external world, can easily flip us into "spiritual bypassing" mode, where we begin to focus on using our gifts as a "quick fix" for everything we don't like about our life. But we can also use our intuition to go deeper into our souls, and to look at the pain we are holding onto in our physical, emotional and spiritual bodies.

Connecting to our intuition and experiencing a Spiritual Reactivation is actually an opportunity to look at our shadow. To recognize the parts of our personality we might see as negative or weak and that we hide away. This may be our anger, our jealousy, our desire, our fear, or our feelings of being unlovable or "not enough." We all have a shadow, even if we see ourselves as happy or a "good person." Society has conditioned us to see certain traits as "bad" and to focus on the "lighter" ones. But we all embody both sides of the coin and it's time for us to embrace this.

Personally, this shadow work gave me insight into unconscious beliefs about myself that led me to self-sabotage and stay small, and allowed me to look at past trauma from childhood and my adult life. ∞ then led me to look at healing my "Ancestor Story." This concept first showed up in my one-on-one sessions with clients, when I was able to see that the blocks and themes showing up in our lives were often the same as those experienced by our ancestors before us. I was then shown a practice for how to identify and, more importantly, heal them. When we acknowledge and heal these blocks, we aren't just healing ourselves but our ancestors before us *and* the future generations to come. It was a game changer for me when I discovered what my Ancestor Story theme was.

Throughout this book, I'll be inviting you to consider what this part of the journey means for you, too, and to look deeply at what's holding you back. Rather than simply asking your intuition what the *future* holds, this is about feeling into any pain and discomfort you may be experiencing in the present moment, and learning to trust in your inner power to heal. I think of this as the practice of "Conscious Intuition."

On a deeper level, cultivating Conscious Intuition means understanding that we are each a unique expression of the collective energy of the planet, and that while we live our lives as individuals, we can impact and be impacted by the energy of the whole. Living from this place, we begin to understand that each and every action creates a ripple effect, and that the more aligned we are with our inner guidance, the more we can have a positive impact in the world. The fact that intuition, crystals, and other spiritual practices are being embraced by the mainstream like never before, tells me that more and more of us are ready to tap into and contribute to this collective energy. The transformational potential for our planet in these times is unprecedented—but we must try not to feel overwhelmed that the task is too big, that there's not enough time, or that change isn't possible. Above all, it's time to change the narrative that change is out of our hands and decisions can only be made by the elite or world governing powers.

I believe we are standing at a planetary crossroads, where we can either continue on a path of destruction, or consciously choose a new way. The fact you are here shows that you are feeling this too. From political tensions, to abuses of power, and the environmental crisis, looking at the chaos in the world around us, you could say that the planet is undergoing its own Spiritual Reactivation, as the shadow parts of our collective are being brought up to be healed. We must remember that this is a vital part of the process, and that us being guided back to our gifts is less about manifesting a perfect partner or a six-figure salary, and more in service of a deep shift within the collective.

What role does intuition play in all this? As the patterns of the past crumble so that we can all transform, it will become your guiding light. It will support you in practicing discernment with your thoughts, words, and deeds, and therefore your impact in the world. It will remind you not to feed on the fear we see in the news and on social media. And it will give you the inner strength, hope, and faith that any uncertainty we're moving through is for the greater good.

When we learn to truly work with our intuition, we can anchor into our bodies for grounding and reclaim our Energetic Self-Sovereignty. We begin to embody a deep presence and alignment with ourselves and with the world around us. Rather than resisting change, we learn how to lean into the chaos. Above all, we come to truly understand that we are part of something greater than ourselves, and that each and every one of our lives has the power to bring about positive change. You don't need to "know" the specifics of your impact; you being YOU is all that's required.

Maybe you think this sounds cheesy or idealistic. Or maybe you feel like you've heard this all before, and are frustrated that nothing seems to be changing. But the shift lies in being guided, right now, to show up for ourselves and each other with a different frequency. This means that it is time to trust your truth. To take back your power. And to remember that

∞

1

THE SPIRITUAL REACTIVATION

You're probably itching to dive straight into the practical steps to connect to your intuition. But before we get there, it's important to acknowledge the journey that most people experience when they are ready to reconnect to their intuitive gifts. I call it the "Spiritual Reactivation." Please don't freak out about me using the word "spiritual" here. I'm not going to reference anything religious. Rather, the Spiritual Reactivation heralds a return to our inner power, a deeper connection to the meaning of our life, and our relationship to who we are in the world.

As you read through the following pages, notice which themes you most identify with or relate to. The stories that make your tummy clench up and cause your skin to prickle. At the end of this chapter and every chapter in this book you will also find an INTUITION IN ACTION section —which is where you will find practical tools, steps and practices to guide you to unlock the learning from each chapter. Don't feel like you need to rush this first step (or any part of this process). Take your time to reflect on all you have experienced in your life so far, and to feel into what comes up for you personally.

WHY A "REACTIVATION"?

You might have heard people in the Spiritual or New Age community talk about going through a "spiritual awakening." This awakening can happen following a health crisis, the ending of a relationship, the loss of a job, or any time you undergo a traumatic life experience that challenges you are intuitive. At the time, you feel a loss of control as your life seems to crumble around you. But there is also a sense that this chaos is waking you up, and a feeling of being more connected to ∞, your gifts, and the world around you. To use the word "awakening" for these kinds of experiences, suggests this is the first time you've felt connected to the spiritual side of life. That all of a sudden, you've been gifted with a "new" way of being. But when it comes to intuition, this isn't the case. Your gifts have always been there, and now external circumstances have triggered a *reactivation* of what has been lying dormant in you all along.

We also think about a spiritual awakening as an "aha" moment: when the clouds part, the light shines down from heaven, and suddenly you feel aligned, connected, and grounded. Now everything makes sense, and you see that there is a spiritual solution to all your earthly problems. But what we rarely hear about is the often confusing and messy process of coming back into alignment with your gifts. It's not all love and light. A spiritual reactivation can be challenging, as it forces you to look at your shadow, to go inwards, and get real about what's not working in your life.

It's not something you can plan or force to happen either. It's not like you can call ∞ up and be like: "Okay yeah, I'd like to apply for my next big life shake-up please. I want to experience this awakening people are talking about, and ideally before I turn 30." Your reactivation will happen when your soul is good and ready—and usually *not* on your preferred schedule. If you've picked up this book it's probably a good sign that you're going through a reactivation right now, have experienced one recently but didn't realize what was happening, or have been through a reactivation and are still on the journey of processing and integrating it. I went through my own reactivation in my late twenties, but it can happen in your teens, twenties, thirties, forties and even later in life. When it happens is personal to you. And it means your soul is ready to graduate from whichever part of your personal curriculum you've been working through.

HOW DO I KNOW IT'S HAPPENING TO ME?

As described above, a Spiritual Reactivation is usually triggered when we're faced with a period of difficulty or uncertainty. A health crisis. Family troubles. The end of a relationship. The loss of a job. We typically experience just one main reactivation event in our lives, and it occurs when we think we've lost something, when something gets taken away from us, or when we experience a monumental, unprecedented challenge. No human being is immune to these circumstances, which show up to lead us into the depths of the shadow of our hidden emotional life and to confront our deepest fears.

For example, faced with the perceived loss of self that can follow any kind of ending, we may find ourselves asking: *"Who am I without X? What really lights me up? What is life all about anyway?"* Seeking the answers to questions like these is a cathartic and mystical process. This becomes a Spiritual Reactivation when it forces us to acknowledge what we know to be true in the deepest, most essential part of ourselves, beyond logic and social conditioning. It is powerful, it is life changing, but by no means is it all rainbows and unicorn magic.

YOU ARE READY

If this sounds daunting, remember:

You are ready to reactivate your gifts.
You are ready to connect to your truth.
You are being called to return to a part of yourself,
That has always been there.
Your Soul is ready to evolve.

◇◇◇◇◇

My reactivation happened in my late twenties and was triggered by a series of losses. It began at age 28 when my parents got divorced after over 30 years of marriage. Not something I ever thought would happen. For some reason I thought that once I was out of my teens we were in the clear, a happy family forever. So when my mum called to let me know what was happening, suddenly everything I thought I valued and wanted for my own future was brought into question. I was in a long-term relationship at the time, and had dreams of marriage and babies in the not too distant future. But did I even want to get married? What if you dedicated your life to someone and it ended? Was marriage worth the risk?

The next shockwave hit not long after the divorce was finalized. As I approached the big 3-0, my own five-year relationship imploded. He ended it, telling me he loved me but didn't see a long-term future with me anymore. I'd been pressuring him to commit to the marriage and the babies, as I'd always assumed I'd be "settled down" by age 30. I wanted that commitment from him so badly, but he didn't feel the same way. I was devastated, and again found myself questioning everything. We'd created a life together. Now our dreams and visions of the future we wanted to create were gone. At the time, it felt as if nothing made sense, but looking back, none of this was coming from out of the blue. *I'd actually been receiving messages and signs from ∞ that the relationship was over, which I'd been choosing to ignore for a really long time.*

I like to say that ∞ will throw mini pebbles in your path to let you know if you've veered off course. But if you're not listening, they'll throw you larger rocks to get your attention and help you course correct. If you're *still* not listening, in come the crushing life boulders to stop you in your tracks. And in this relationship, the road had already been bumpy.

It began when my basement bedroom in a shared apartment in South West London was completely flooded by a freak storm on a hot, summer's day. That same week I was also robbed walking home from the station. Two days later he broke it off. I should have listened to my intuition—this was a sign that he didn't really care about my well-being. To make things worse, I also found out he'd been cheating on me, something I'd suspected and had been ignoring, simply because I didn't want it to be true.

You'd have thought these were large enough "rocks" to make me start off down a different path. But we got back together eight months later. We had a few more happy years together, and life was good. We were both expanding in our careers, enjoying life, and making plans. But I knew in my heart something still wasn't right. He would feel cold and distant at times, pulling away as I drew closer. I held onto any brief moments of connection, hoping these would outweigh the times where I felt the rift between us. I saw the potential for deep love in his heart space. But he kept it so protected. Looking back, I can see that the healer in me had made it my mission to try and crack his heart open. Did it work? No. I knew I deserved more, and felt I'd become someone else to fit into the relationship. I'd even started to put "leave" dates in my calendar on my phone; as in, if it's not better by this date ... then I'll leave. But these dates came and went and I stayed put.

Time for ∞ to roll out the boulders, in the form of two major "random" accidents in our home that triggered the process of us finally breaking up for good. The first was another flooding! Our basement flat in London flooded from heavy rain, with sewer water everywhere. Our flat needed new floors and had to be repainted, the inconvenience putting the relationship under strain as we began to bicker and turn on each other. At the time I found myself asking, "Why do I keep getting flooded? What is this trying to say to me?" I can now see that the flooding symbolized the washing away of what was stopping me from being my authentic self: in this case a deadend relationship. Since I had ignored previous signs, ∞ brought in destruction and chaos to kick-start my reactivation and my connection back to my inner truth.

But still I didn't leave. Which meant ∞ had to throw a final boulder to get our attention. This time it literally woke us up. We were fast asleep when a car crashed into our apartment at 6am in the morning. I'll never forget the noise of brick caving in and the smell of burnt rubber; the dread seeping in as I pictured somebody dead at the wheel in our living room. Luckily the car hadn't gone all the way into the apartment, but there was extensive damage (the driver fled the scene). The tension and arguments following the crash, as we dealt with insurers and managed the extensive repairs, led to the end of the relationship. I was an emotional wreck trying to keep it all together, literally crying on the bathroom floor, questioning why this was happening to me. Moving back in with my Mum, both of us single, was not what I'd envisioned to mark the beginning of my thirties.

You'd think that would have been it for rock bottoms in 2012, but turns out it was also time for ∞ to clear out what wasn't working in my career. At the time I was a department head for a film production company, where I loved the process of seeing creative ideas brought to life. I'd joined the company because it seemed progressive, expansive and a fun place to work. But what I actually experienced was poor communication and intense internal power struggles. In the nine months I was there, I was asked to consider what kind of environment I wanted to work in, and what business values were important to me. Ultimately, I was let go and I went freelance. I was told I could have fought for wrongful dismissal, but I just wanted a clean break. I was done with messy breakups. But I was also confused, frustrated, and angry. Again, I found myself asking why this was all happening to me at once. My family being broken apart. The end of my relationship. And now the loss of a job I had fought so hard for.

I felt as if my whole world was disintegrating around me, and as if the emotional support system I had been able to rely on no longer existed. Only with hindsight, having gone on a healing journey using my intuition as a guide, I am now able to see that these endings were actually beginnings. That ultimately, this was the start of my journey to discover who "Natalie" is beyond everything I thought I knew about myself. Life events forced me to pause and go inward. To look at what was really important to me and what I needed to let go. A process that was the beginning of my Spiritual Reactivation.

What's interesting, is that this all happened in 2012—a year that many in the spiritual community had been predicting would bring a powerful collective shift in the global consciousness, as December 21st 2012 was the last date to be depicted by the ancient Mayan calendar. There was plenty of media hype about the "end of the world," with Doomsday theories flying around. I had the privilege of seeing the sunrise on December 21st (the Winter Solstice) with my back leaning on the magical prehistoric stones of Stonehenge in England—a special day I'll never forget. I went with my Mum, my Aunt and our friend Evelyn, who also attended those first ever psychic circles I went to when I was 16. We decided to go because we wanted to mark the moment and celebrate this passage of time.

We arrived in darkness, a crowd already gathering, full of excitement

about being so close to the sacred stones on this special date. The atmosphere was electric with the loud sound of drumming and singing, with
many wearing traditional druid clothing and carrying fire torches. In that
moment, I felt a part of myself come home. I now know that what I experienced was a return to my intuitive gifts, as if my human being was being reintegrated with my soul. As the sun rose over the stones for the first
time in the wake of all these endings, I felt a sense of hope, and was able
to see the world with new eyes. I began to believe in my own self worth
again, and as if, no matter what I was facing in the external world, I had
the inner strength to come through it.

WHERE WERE YOU IN 2012?

In the years since this auspicious date, I believe individuals everywhere have experienced our own personal reactivations so we can
show up for a larger, collective Spiritual Reactivation that is under-
way. Journal on the below prompts and see what comes up...

- What did you experience in your life around this time, and how do
  you think this is connected to your spiritual reactivation?
- What themes were present in 2012 that are often repeated in the
  challenges you face?
- What life changes did you feel called to make during this time?
- What have you learned about leaning into uncertainty on the
  path to living your truth?

YOUR REACTIVATION: WHAT ARE THE SIGNS?

When we experience a Spiritual Reactivation it can affect us physically,
emotionally, and in the way we see the world around us. In the moment, it
can also be hard to see what's happening—all you know is life feels overwhelming and nothing seems to make sense. This next section will walk
you through some of the reactivation symptoms you might be in the midst
of right now, have already been through, or are about to experience. You
might be surprised how many you can relate to.

PHYSICAL SYMPTOMS

When I went through my reactivation, I actually went to a doctor to see if there was something medically wrong with me. When the tests came back saying I was fit and healthy, I was confused; the physical symptoms I was experiencing felt so real. I wish I'd had this list to refer to at the time, as it would've helped me diagnose my situation—and I still experience some of these symptoms now when my gifts are being upgraded.

IMPORTANT: If you are experiencing any of these symptoms and you are concerned please ALSO go and seek proper advice from a trained medical professional.

Energy or pressure at the top of your head. This means your crown chakra is being reactivated. Chakras are energy points located all over the body. Traditionally the crown chakra, located at the top of your head, represents the flow of energy between ∞ and the connection to your true self. When you feel pressure here, you are opening up this energy portal to receive information from ∞ and reactivate a connection in your energetic intuitive body.

Energy or pressure in the Third Eye space. If the space in between your eyebrows is tingling, buzzing or feeling sore, it shows that you are reactivating your intuitive gifts. The third eye chakra or pineal gland has traditionally been associated with "seeing gifts." With this third eye tingle you might also experience sensitivity to light.

Brain fog. You may lose thoughts and not feel super clear. This is connected to the influx of new energy that is coming through the crown chakra and third eye energy points as you reactivate your gifts.

Buzzing in the ears. I thought I had tinnitus at one point—but it was ∞ reactivating my "hearing gifts" (more on what these are in a later chapter).

Heightened senses. You may have a stronger sense of smell, see colors more vividly, or be disturbed by small noises you never noticed before.

Again, this is ∞ reactivating your sensory gifts.

Bodily changes. You may feel bloated and experience weight gain or loss. As you begin to reactivate your gifts, you may need to physically adjust to the new energy that you're connecting to. Our bodies can take time to recalibrate to the new frequencies they are experiencing. When I first had my reactivation I felt bloated, which highlighted to me all the things in my life I was holding onto and not letting go of.

Dizziness. This can feel like vertigo, and I found putting a blanket over your head really helps as it covers your crown chakra and can help lessen the dizziness. This again is connected to the influx of new energy that is coming through the crown chakra and third eye energy points as you reactivate your gifts. Even now, I can experience dizziness when my gifts are upgrading or I'm receiving lots of intuitive guidance.

Heart palpitations. You may feel your heart fluttering as this energy begins to reactivate the intuitive heart. Although the third eye has historically been identified as the space of intuition in the body, the heart is really where our intuitive power truly lies (I'll be sharing more on this later, too).

Food intolerances or change in diet. You may suddenly find you can't stomach certain foods, such as dairy or gluten. Your relationship to alcohol or sugar may change as your body can't process toxins like it used to. You may feel called to give up meat products. As we reactivate our gifts we may also be shown what food and substances we have used to numb ourselves to prevent us from connecting to our inner power.

Changes in sleep patterns. You may find you are sleeping more lightly or more deeply. Our bodies regenerate at night so the reactivation process can intensify while we're sleeping. We're also relaxed so our bodies open up more. You might suddenly experience waking up in the night— even waking up at the same time every night.

Vivid dreams. You may find yourself dreaming more and experiencing lucid dreaming, astral travel, or recurring dreams. You may even begin to have what feel like prophetic dreams. We can receive intuitive messages in our dreams so you're being opened up to this, too.

EMOTIONAL SYMPTOMS

When we go through loss, change, and what feel like rock bottom moments during a Spiritual Reactivation, it can bring on a wide range of emotions. You might be feeling super low one day and buzzing with excitement the next. During my Spiritual Reactivation, I struggled with depression to the point that some days I lacked the motivation to get out of bed. In the void between my old life ending and me finding my way onto my true path, I was overwhelmed with confusion about the meaning of life. If you're going through it, please don't do this alone; reach out to a friend, family member, medical practitioner, therapist, or coach. In the meantime, here are some examples of what you may be feeling and the messages from ∞ therein.

Sadness. You are grieving the old you and the life you are leaving behind. It's normal to feel sadness as you reconnect to your intuitive gifts and onto the path to discover your true self.

Anxiety. An increase in the energy flow into your body can lead to feelings of agitation. It can be helpful to reframe any anxiety as an indicator that a new form of energy is entering your intuitive body, opening you up and clearing out energetic blocks. Remind yourself that this will pass.

Depression. You are letting go of the old and being called to begin the healing journey in front of you. You may be feeling overwhelmed as this task seems such a big undertaking. Remember that you are essentially being invited into a journey of self-acceptance, and a return to living from the heart. Try not to fear any big emotions coming up. Find small ways to feel good each day. Call on people for support, especially if you're feeling alone.

Unexplained anger. Anger may bubble up as you question, "WHY IS THIS HAPPENING TO ME?!" You might be angry towards yourself, towards others you perceive as having triggered difficult challenges, and towards the collective as a whole. Try not to repress any anger during this time. Acknowledge the anger and start to process it by writing it down, talking to someone, or literally "shaking" it out of your body.

Feeling "stuck." As the reactivation unfolds you may find yourself feeling stuck between the life you're leaving behind and wondering what the "future you" is going to look like. In these moments, try to focus on simply being in the present. Ask yourself, what am I being called to heal *right now?*

Loneliness and isolation. A reactivation can make us feel alone and separated from the people around us. It can feel like we are the only ones going through this experience. Even if you don't feel supported, trust that ∞ and your Ancestors (who we'll meet in a little bit) are supporting you during this process. Try and be around friends, family and people you love when it feels aligned for you.

Fear. The big F-word can hold you back from stepping fully and confidently into your worth, your power, and your truth. Remember that fear is simply a reminder that you are on a deep transformational journey where you will no longer play small. Lean into the fear: it's actually going to help you during this reactivation by showing you where in your life you need to step into your power.

Anticipation. During the reactivation you might feel excitable, exhilarated, and full of energy. Trust that these emotions are here to help you as you begin to return to your inner power and truth. On the days you feel this, look at what you'd like to call into your life and what changes you want to bring forward, and take action with this energy.

Joy. As shifts occur and you feel ∞ at work in your life, you may experience a flood of joyful feelings in your body. You might not be able to pinpoint why, but there is a deep feeling of gratitude and appreciation for the world around you. This is a sure-fire sign that you are returning to your gifts.

Unconditional love. As the intuitive heart space opens and you begin to reactivate this energy portal the feelings of unconditional love can be overwhelming. You might have never experienced this level of love before. Simply allow it to flow through your body and don't try and resist feeling this love. You deserve to feel it. You are love.

SPIRITUAL SYMPTOMS

Not only are there physical and emotional symptoms of a reactivation but "spiritual" ones too. These highlight to us that we're reconnecting to the spiritual parts of ourselves that have been lying dormant. This sounds magical, and it is—but spiritual symptoms can also involve increased awareness of any pain, suffering and shadow. It can feel as if a mask is falling away, peeling back the layers as the truth is revealed to you. Trust what you are experiencing, and commit to investigating any questions that come up for you.

Seeing the world for the first time. You may feel like you're finally seeing everything for what it really is, in your relationships, in your community, and in our larger society. As well as the wonder and the new possibilities, taking off the rose tinted glasses also means becoming more aware of pain and suffering, and gaining a deeper understanding of systemic oppression and of human beings' impact on the planet. Commit to staying conscious of it all.

New perceptions. You might notice the small details of the world around you with fresh eyes. Colors and textures may seem more vivid, and you may be more aware of the beauty that is all around you in nature, in your city, and in your home.

Feeling more connected and present. As your intuitive gifts kick in, you will become more aware of the synchronicities, signs and symbols that show up in your life to guide you. As you begin to pay attention and trust in these messages, you will start to feel more confident and become aware that you are tuning in to your inner power.

Heightened sense of being part of the collective. You realize that you're part of something bigger and that everything you do has an impact on the collective. You may feel greater social responsibility as you connect to the world's injustices. You may want to take a stand, voice your opinions, and take part.

Heightened empathy. You notice you are more able to tap into other people's feelings, emotions and energy, and how this impacts you. Being around lots of people might feel overwhelming—and I'll be sharing tools and practices so you don't have to take on the energy of others in the next chapter.

Craving authentic relationships. You may feel disconnected from friendships and relationships that once worked as you desire deeper connections. Gossip and small talk no longer appeals to you. This is part of the shadow being revealed to you, as you are shown the relationships that have blocked you from being your authentic self.

Craving alone time. You may need more time alone, to be with your own thoughts and switch off from the outside world. If you're traditionally an extrovert who loves being around people this may take you by surprise, but this shows you are ready to re-learn to be comfortable in your own skin. Discovering who you are means you no longer need the approval of others for validation.

Questioning your purpose. You might realize what you do for work or pleasure no longer lights you up. You might begin to question what truly brings you joy and happiness, and even wonder about your role on the planet. These realizations show you where you have been playing small, holding yourself back from your inner desires, dreams and passions. You

ven be called to return to an idea or vision of something you have
s wanted to have or do in your life. Trust whatever is coming up for
you. Listen to your heart's calling.

If you're feeling overwhelmed by any of these symptoms, I want to
stress that they do go away. They are simply the side effects of an upgrade
to your inner operating system. But when you're in the middle of a reactivation, you may find yourself asking: Is there something wrong with me?
The answer is that nothing is wrong. In fact, everything is very right.

YOUR REACTIVATION

Take a moment to note down each of the reactivation symptoms
you have been experiencing.

- Have you experienced or are currently experiencing any of the
  PHYSICAL reactivation symptoms? List which ones.
- Have you felt or are currently feeling any of the EMOTIONAL re-
  activation symptoms? List which ones.
- Have you felt or are currently feeling any of the SPIRITUAL reac-
  tivation symptoms? List which ones.

If you are experiencing a Spiritual Reactivation right now, what do
you think the symptoms you identified are trying to tell you about
yourself during this time? If you have already had a spiritual reactivation reflect on what the symptoms you listed above taught you
about yourself.

My personal reactivation journey taught me that I needed to take it
all day by day, and to flow with what was happening. It was when I re-
sisted the changes that the symptoms seemed to intensify, but as I surrendered and trusted that everything was unfolding exactly how it was
supposed to, I felt so much better. Each morning, I checked in to see how
I was feeling emotionally, physically and spiritually. Some days I would
feel super energized and then be exhausted by the afternoon. Other days
I just wanted to shut myself off from the outside world. On these intense

emotional low days I kept trusting that this would pass. I noticed that it helped to stay in the present as much as possible, instead of tripping into the future. I also found that singing, exercise, dance, or yoga, allowed intense emotions and reactivation energy to move through my body. Below in the "Intuitive Action" section I share some practical tools for how you can stay present as you navigate your Spiritual Reactivation.

And please don't worry, you won't experience these symptoms on a daily basis as you learn how to connect to your intuitive gifts. However, you may find them recurring any time you're going through an upgrade or recalibration in your life. It actually wasn't until I wrote out these symptoms that I realized I'm going through an upgrade of my gifts right now. Because there is no end point to this journey. Once we say "yes" to living in alignment with our gifts, we're continually evolving and becoming more us. "Waking up" is one thing, but living from an activated place is about to become your new normal.

◇◇◇◇◇

INTUITIVE ACTION

- Keep a journal during any period of Spiritual Reactivation. I didn't and I wish I could look back at the events that were unfolding and how I felt about them in more detail. Writing down the physical, emotional, and spiritual symptoms of your reactivation may help you to make sense of what you're experiencing—even if it's only in retrospect.

- At the end of your day, write down three things that you feel grateful for and that you appreciate about your life. This will help you to gain perspective of what *is* working in your life, however small, during this intense transformation.

- Try and stay in the present moment as much as possible. Move your body. Head into nature. Listen to music. Eat your favorite food. Have a bath. Put on a favourite item of clothing. Read. Watch a movie. Paint. Draw. Connect to activities you intuitively feel might bring you joy.

- Call in support to help you during this process, in the form of friends, family, a therapist or healer. You are not alone.

- Take rest instead of action if that's what you're being intuitively called to. Sometimes doing nothing is the action.

- Listen or watch my Reactivation Guided Meditation. This guided meditation has been channeled from Spirit to help you reactivate your gifts, and you can find it in the online portal.

REPEAT TO SUPPORT YOUR SPIRITUAL REACTIVATION

You will find a special "invocation" in each chapter of this book. These are designed to be read out loud and repeated to invoke the teachings of each chapter. The energy of your voice is power-ful, and saying these words will help them imprint in your energetic intuitive body. Speak them whenever you feel called to. Sing them in the shower. Say them in your head while you go on a walk. Use them any way you feel intuitively called to do so. By repeating this invocation you are declaring to ∞ that you're ready to access and reactivate your gifts.

I am transforming
I am reactivating
I am returning home to my intuitive gifts

I trust the unfolding journey
I surrender what I am releasing and letting go
I am here to live in alignment with my true self

I am transforming
I am reactivating
I am stepping into my intuitive power

∞

2

WHAT'S HOLDING YOU BACK?

You might not be consciously aware of it but you have been imprinted with deep programming that has taught you to fear your intuition. Ultimately, this conditioning has been preventing you from trusting and accessing your gifts and living as your full self. As we begin on this journey it's important for you to look at the exact nature of what is holding you back, so that you can move it out of your body and your psyche, move past any fear, and take back your power.

In the introduction, I explained how ancestral shame about our intuition has been passed from generation to generation under the control of the patriarchy, Western religious sects and colonialism. Stemming from a period in history when witches went into hiding and intuitives were killed for using their gifts, the fear and shame associated with this mass execution has been passed on through your DNA without you even realizing. Not to mention it being reinforced by societal messages about this work being "woo woo," not "real" or not relevant to the world we live in today. Stored in your physical, emotional and spiritual body, this trauma is showing up *right now* as any fears, doubts and anxieties you may feel about connecting to your intuition.

In order for you to release this, we must first discover the nature of your personal fears, and the beliefs they are connected to. Until you go through this process, trying to access your intuition will be like buying a brand new computer or smartphone and discovering it's got an outdated operating system that needs to be upgraded before you can begin to use it. Think of it like an intuition reset!

WHAT WILL OTHER PEOPLE THINK?

Whether you've never connected to your intuition before or you've already been experimenting with your gifts, some fears have most likely come up around what other people will have to say about it. Perhaps you're afraid they won't take you seriously, or that you'll be judged as being weird and woo-woo by friends, family members and your wider community. During the witch trials many who were arrested and killed were turned in to the authorities by the people closest to them. This Ancestor Story manifests in a fear that our loved ones may turn against us or deceive us. Instead of shining our gifts brightly we hide them away, out of sight from others.

It's also known that during this period of genocide, women turned on other intuitive women in order to save themselves. This ancestral patterning can still show up today as women being super mean and critical, and pulling each other down—a conditioned behaviour orchestrated by the patriarchy as a way to keep women disempowered. Instead of one unified, powerful force, who bonded together to support each other, they were turned against each other.

This has been part of my own journey. Even before I'd attended my first psychic circle, I'd experienced judgment from other girls in my school. At age fourteen, I felt confident in myself but struggled to fit in among the different social groups in my class. I never felt quite like I belonged. One lunchtime some girls suggested we do a Ouija board, inspired by the witchy 1990s movie "The Craft." We were nervous as we set up a makeshift board on a school desk and we all thought nothing would happen because "it only happens in the movies!" But sure enough, the paper cup from the school canteen started to move and spell out answers to our questions. One girl looked at me, fear splashed across her face, and accused me of pushing it and making it happen. The other girls all chimed in shouting, "Stop moving it, Natalie!" The cup was moving all by itself. I didn't understand why back then, but I was left feeling confused, judged, and ashamed.

Sometimes this shame simply manifests as a deep knowing in the body. A feeling that if you do put your gifts out into the open you will be ridiculed or judged. This might happen when you sense a Spirit from the other side trying to get your attention, or you suddenly know or feel something about a situation or a person but you don't want to share it in case people think you're weird. It might not make sense, but suddenly you feel a tightness across your chest, a block in your throat, or anxiety in your stomach. Triggering ancestral memories of being punished for using your gifts, in either scenario the body will block you from connecting to your gifts as a safety response.

When have you felt judged by others or that you've had to hide your gifts?
What does this fear/block feel like in your body?
Have you been hiding this book away?
What are you afraid people might say if they knew you were reading it?

WILL MY FAMILY STILL ACCEPT ME?

We've all experienced different upbringings, and the beliefs, moral codes, and value systems of our families of origin or early caregivers can inhibit us from accessing our own inner truth and guidance system. How and where we are raised can also act as a block. For example, if you were raised in a conservative, religious or intensely disciplined family, town, school, or country, you might have been taught that it was wrong to cultivate your own values, freedom of thought, creativity, and ways to connect to your inner power. But this isn't always the case. What you were taught about ∞, the "other side," ghosts, or magic in your early life, can be an even bigger block.

All children are born into the world fully connected to our gifts, as we haven't yet been conditioned by society or our family to believe that this part of ourselves isn't "normal." This is why children are often uninhibited about talking to their "invisible friends" and sharing their experiences playing in the unseen realms. Childhood intuition also manifests as an ability to read emotions and situations better than most adults—a survival mechanism that helps us navigate the world and get what we need before we have language. But for the majority of us this intuitive intelligence isn't nurtured by our family and wider support system as we get older.

Instead, our gifts are suppressed. We begin to hear things like, "Don't be silly there's nothing there" and "Who are you talking to? People will think you're crazy. Stop that." Or the big one, "That's not *REAL*." We trust our adult caretakers, and so we learn that we are doing something "wrong" when we connect to our gifts. We begin to believe that there is no such thing as magic. The irony being that the grown-ups are simply acting on their own fears or past negative experiences with connecting to ∞. They in turn heard the same from their families or caregivers. And the cycle continues from generation to generation.

Imagine how different our lives would be if intuition was taught in schools. If kids were encouraged to trust their own inner knowing, taught how to decipher their emotions, and guided to see their gifts as normal! What would our society look like? How would we as a collective relate to one another and communicate in a deeper and more open way?

Many intuitive children may also have felt like the "odd one out" in their family. That they didn't measure up in some way, or that they were expected to behave in a way that didn't sit quite right with them. Maybe reading this is bringing up memories of feeling different or alone within your family unit. This is a common experience among people whose gifts have been suppressed, the irony being that we may push our gifts down further in our attempts to "fit in."

Another block to our intuitive power is the pressure to achieve, something that's conditioned into us from an early age. We learn that play, fun, and imagination (all ways to access our intuition) are "childish" and a "waste of time," while creating a structured path to achieving our goals is what will bring "success." This focus on striving for success as the root to happiness and finding "meaning" in our lives is once again part of our white supremacist, abelist, patriarchal programming—not least because it creates more good little worker bees to keep feeding the system, rather than pursuing our own creativity and gifts. Yep, that's right! More systemic programming to limit us from accessing our intuitive power and living our truth.

Notice how in the above scenario, the message is that power lies somewhere *outside* of us—is something that can be attained by working hard, notching up accolades, and earning lots of money. How we're told that success is also an external thing, based on what job we have, the size of our bank balance, the house we live in, or our relationship status. All of this only deters us from looking *within* for the answers to what truly makes us powerful, while keeping us in a constant, and often exhausting, state of doing and achieving.

Do you remember seeing or experiencing ∞ as a child?
Were you encouraged to develop this side of yourself?
Did you feel like the "odd one" growing up?
Do you feel pressure to be successful?
What does success mean to you?

INTUITION IS THE DEVIL'S WORK

Many organized religions teach that to connect to your intuition and inner power is the Devil's work, and that by opening this portal you will attract negative entities and expose yourself to darkness and evil. After all, most organized religions teach that ∞ also exists *outside* of us, in God or another deity, and that for us to access the power, truth and guidance of ∞, we must turn our will over to the hands of God (or, rather, the appointed church officials who have access to "him"). The Western religious sects played a major role in the mass killing of intuitives and witches during the 14th-17th Centuries, which was orchestrated in an attempt to take control over what we believed, who we worshipped, and how we practiced our faith. This was also part of the white European colonization of Africa, Asia, Oceania and the Americas, as the indigenous people of these continents were forced to "convert" to Christianity and turn away from their own spiritual practices and deities. This control mechanism still shows up in society today and, especially if we were raised in a religious family (as mentioned above), can be a big block to us accessing our gifts.

For millennia humans have been connecting to a higher power. Have turned to something greater than ourselves to find meaning and make sense of our human existence. Our intuition is one way to forge this connection, and this is blocked when we believe that we can only experience "spirituality" as part of organized religion—with all of its rules and hierarchies.

But you can be religious *and* intuitive. With discernment and an ability to see beyond fear-based programming and control, it is possible to believe in God or another external power AND have access to your intuitive gifts. This means acknowledging that the path to ∞, resides *inside* each and every one of us. That we are all born with VIP access.

On the flip-side, if you were brought up atheist you might have been taught to believe that there is nothing spiritual in the world—only science and rational thought. In this case, it might be a stretch to even imagine a "higher power" or to think of your intuition as being in any way spiritual. For you, a block to accessing your gifts may show up as scepticism or a need to explain "how it works." This journey to reconnect to your intuition is all about being open to guiding yourself back to your inner wisdom, knowledge and power.

What was your experience of religion growing up?
What memories do you have of being told that connecting to ∞ was a bad thing?
In what ways can a person be both religious and intuitive?
Do you believe in a higher power?

IS IT EVEN SAFE?

This is one of the biggest blocks to connecting to your intuition—stemming from religious teachings, ancestral memories of the witch trials ... and good old-fashioned horror movies depicting evil spirits, haunted houses, and people being possessed and acting "crazy." And let's be blunt: yes, there are negative energies in the Spirit realm that you may be exposed to when using your intuition. But you can also learn how to protect yourself, set clear intentions about how you work with ∞, and, most importantly, trust yourself to use your own power to call in only what you *want* to connect to.

This fear is also a symptom of current societal programming that tells us we shouldn't want to know or look at the more shadowy, scary parts of ourselves or society. That we should just focus on the "high-vibe, love and light" aspects of our nature and the world. But connecting to our intuition is about learning to work WITH all of our shadowy parts we try and hide away or don't feel safe looking at. They co-exist together and we can experience a powerful transformation when we embody all parts of ourselves.

You may feel a spike in anxiety and fear just reading this. Perhaps you've had an experience with a negative energy or something freaked you out when you opened yourself up and now you're afraid to go there again. Please don't worry. The fact you're even here shows you are ready to release this old programming, and there's a whole chapter coming up on how you can access your gifts in a way that feels safe, empowered, and aligned with all that ∞ wants to show you.

What are you scared you might connect to?
What bad or negative experiences are you ready to release?
What scary images come up when you think of going to the "other side" and what can you replace these with?

DO I HAVE TO SAY I'M A "PSYCHIC"?

Something else that can hold you back from embracing your gifts is fear around the word *psychic*. There is actually no difference between the labels "psychic" and "intuitive"—they mean the same thing. But even as spirituality becomes more mainstream, the word psychic still has a huge stigma attached. We've been told that psychics are fake, are out to take our money, and put curses on people when we don't pay up. Of course, as in any business there are people operating with different levels of professionalism and integrity out there—and just as there are dishonest doctors, untrustworthy lawyers or shady tradespeople (not to mention some of our world leaders!), less than scrupulous intuitives have given the practice a bad name.

But the truth is we are all "psychic." We all work with our intuition differently and with different levels of skill. For some of us it might come more naturally and for others it might take a bit more practice. But we can all access our intuition, you don't have to label it one thing or another, and it is always to empower you.

What do you like or not like about the word psychic?
Does it bring up fear for you? What are those fears?
Do you resonate more with being intuitive or being psychic?

BUT, GOOGLE ...

We have been trained to place so much trust in external guidance, especially with the advent of technology, that we have become fearful of trusting ourselves. When was the last time you drove or walked around your city without looking at the GPS on your phone? When you decided where you were going and simply trusted you knew the right way. Do you know by memory the road layout of your city? Or do you default to GPS, even though you know *roughly* where you're going?

And then there's good old Google. How often when you know something to be true do you *still* do a search just to check and make sure? Plenty of us also rely on Google to tell us the meaning of our dreams, as well as to decipher the signs and symbols that are actually our intuition in action. The same way some religions have taught us to believe that ∞ exists outside of ourselves, technology encourages us to place our trust in external sources versus consulting with our own ancient *intuitive technology*.

Imagine what it would feel like not to rely on Google for answers. To navigate through your day using just your inner guidance system—just like our ancestors did as they connected intuitively to the stars in the night sky. Given the rapid advances of technology in the 21st Century, it's something we've come to depend on very quickly, presenting a very modern block to us accessing our gifts. It's so easy to type a question into Google, and the answer comes back instantly. We want answers quick and fast. We feel we haven't got time to wait. This can be helpful when the car breaks down and you need an auto repair, or you're in a new area and want some local tips. But our addiction to instant gratification disconnects us from our power, as we don't want to invest the time it takes to develop our intuition and trust our *own* truths. Yes, technology has so many benefits. But we need to remember that we also have access to deep inner knowing, and that if we don't use it, we're in danger of losing it.

How do you feel if you leave the house without your phone?
How heavily do you rely on Google and GPS for guidance?
Imagine how you would navigate your day without these things. How does this feel?

INTUITION AND MENTAL HEALTH

If you suffer from anxiety or depression a big question might be lurking: *"How is my anxiety or depression going to impact me connecting to my gifts?"* After all, by going on this journey to reactivate your intuition you are also forging a deeper connection with your feelings and emotions. This in itself might be bringing up fear and anxiety as you question whether you are even ready to step into your power. Trust that these thoughts are "normal"—and that connecting to your intuition might actually help with any symptoms you've been experiencing. Your intuition isn't going to be a "cure" but it *is* here to support you.

There's also a misconception that you won't be able to access your gifts if you're on anxiety medication or antidepressants, as if they are numbing you in some way. This isn't the case. Don't feel like you have to come off your medication to connect to your intuition. Simply work with the exercises, tools, and meditations in this book, and go slow with yourself. If you need the medication, don't feel guilty about taking it. Trust where you're at and what your body is asking of you so you can live your life and heal.

If you do feel called to come off any medication please seek the guidance and help of a trained medical professional to help you navigate this.

Do you suffer from anxiety and depression?
Have you felt that your mental health has impacted your intuition in the past? In what ways?
Are you concerned that this will impact your ability to connect with your gifts?

PEOPLE PLEASING AND FITTING IN

We've become a collective of people pleasers, worried about saying something out of turn, and desperate to fit in. Even when we do get an intuitive message to do something, change something, or speak up, how many of us stop ourselves from taking action on the intuitive hit because of this need to please? Even if our whole body is screaming at us, social conditioning to be nice and not rock the boat means it still feels easier to keep a smile on your face and respond with "I'm great, thanks!" if anybody asks. And "cancel culture" has made this even worse. Even with so much going on in the world politically and socially, when you are terrified of being shut down or attacked, it can feel like it's easier not to share your beliefs and inner knowing.

I want you to think about how many times you have kept quiet out of fear or wanting to be liked, whether it's been in your relationships, your work life, or within your community. Now visualize everybody in the collective. How many of us are holding back from expressing how we really feel, and as such ignoring our intuitive guidance, out of people-pleasing and a need to fit in? Now think about our world leaders and the people who shape our politics and policies. How many of *them* are not speaking their personal truths or the truths of the people they represent to fit in with the current establishments, stay in favor, and keep hold of the power? That's a lot of people! Which means a lot of suppressed intuitive action in the world.

When we people please and don't show up authentically we step out of our personal power. We want to feel more connected to people and yet we fear rejection. But wouldn't you rather be accepted by a small group who see ALL of you and allow you to stay in YOUR POWER rather than suppress who you really are to be liked by everybody? Speaking our intuitive truths is part of this process, and actually allows for deeper, more authentic bonds. When we do this in our personal lives this energy ripples out in the wider collective—in quitting the people pleasing and staying true to you, you give others permission to do the same.

In what ways are you a people pleaser?
When in your life have you wanted to do something, change something or say something in your life but didn't take action on it out of people pleasing and fitting in?

⬥⬥⬥⬥⬥

Are you beginning to see how easy it is to fear your intuition? And how society and its rules, beliefs, and indoctrinations about the nature of "Spirit" have likely been a big part of this? Not that working to remove these fears and blocks will be an overnight job, making it feel safe to instantly wear your intuitive gifts on your sleeve. But by reading this book and opting into this work, you are choosing to rewrite your narrative around this. This is your journey and yours alone, which means it's important to take it at your own pace and do what feels right for you. But as challenging as it might feel sometimes, it is only when you identify your blocks and work to move past them, that you can truly take back your inner power. This process will allow ∞ to flow into back into your body, as you open the intuitive portal.

⬥⬥⬥⬥⬥

INTUITIVE ACTION

Scan back over your answers to the questions for each section. Which fears and blocks to accessing your intuitive gifts came up? Which resonate the most strongly with you? List these out on a separate piece of paper, or on a fresh page in your intuition journal, beginning each sentence with: *"I have been afraid that ..."*

Once you have done this find a mirror and sit or stand in front of it. Read the fears you have listed out loud while looking at yourself. Once you have done this burn what you've written, repeating the invocation for this chapter (below).

GUIDED MEDITATION

To seal this ritual, listen to my Reset and Release Guided Meditation. This guided meditation has been channeled to help you identify and release any fear and shame about connecting to your intuition. You can find it in the online portal.

REPEAT TO INVOKE RELEASING SOCIETAL PROGRAMMING AND BLOCKS

I am intuitive

I am not afraid of the gifts I was born with

I set myself free from my fears and blocks

I release myself from all societal programming stored in my intuitive body

I release all shame and judgment

I release myself from the need to people please

I trust myself and call back my power

I am here

I am intuitive

3

ENERGETIC SELF-SOVEREIGNTY

Our energetic intuitive body is a highly complex system. You can picture it as if you are looking down on a busy city like New York from above, with its labyrinth of streets, lights, and traffic signs, moving millions of people from A to B. Even though you can't see it, you can also visualize the subway trains beneath the city transporting yet more people around. In the same way that everything in this layered city system is connected and interdependent, the energy in your body is connected to your intuitive body, and how they communicate with each other impacts how you connect with the outside world.

This energetic system is also where we connect to our inner power. When we learn to ground and look after our own energy, what I call practicing Energetic Self-Sovereignty, we feel connected, anchored and safe. We can make clear decisions, follow our instincts, and confidently trust our own inner guidance. But since energy is porous and undefined, it is easy for our energy to become enmeshed with the energy of the world around us. It mingles with the energy of our friends, families, colleagues, and takes on the energy of the food we eat, the music we listen to, and what we read in social media and in the news. When you begin to pay attention, you'll notice how we are bombarded almost constantly with external information, thoughts, beliefs, expectations, points of view, and emotional triggers. All of which carry their own energetic imprint.

This means most of us have lost touch with what our own energy feels like, especially those of us who live in cities, where the external energetic noise is at fever pitch. Without you even realizing you may be taking on energy that is affecting your ability to stay in your own power, and pre-venting you from accessing the clarity to make intuitive decisions. You may feel this as anxiety, as if your mind is buzzing on overtime, or as a de-sire to retreat from the outside world. If this sounds like you, don't worry. In this chapter I'm going to teach you how to develop Energetic Self-Sov-ereignty.

You can think of this as being in charge of your own energy—and it's one of the most important skills to practice when it comes to connecting to your intuitive gifts. As mentioned in the last chapter, many of us uncon-sciously shut our intuition down from a fear of connecting to dark energy, bad spirits, or negative entities. But instead of empowering us, this only disconnects us from our inner guidance, leaving us feeling more out of control, unsafe and ungrounded. And while it's true that good boundaries are important, practicing Energetic Self-Sovereignty is also a way of stay-ing open, while standing strong in your truth.

You may have heard traditional New Age communities talk about the practice of "calling in protection." This is spoken about as a precaution before opening ourselves to ∞ and connecting to our intuition. However, the use of the word "protection" can heighten any fears about taking on external energies, suggesting as it does that you need to lock yourself up in an ironclad suit of armor before you open up this part of yourself. That you need to guard yourself *against* negative exterior forces. Can you see how this is actually the opposite of you taking back your power? Any ritu-al or practice that states things have to be done in the correct order, sug-gesting that if you skip a step you're going to attract negative energy, are also based in fear—something that is prevalent in the New Age communi-ty, and which is yet another hangover from the era of the witch trials. Even when the intention is to help people, this kind of messaging only hinders us from truly trusting ourselves and being in control of our own energy.

Yes, negative energy and entities exist (the supernatural kind, and the social media kind), but instead of feeling the need to "protect" ourselves to ward off any potential threat it's time for us to realize we can be proactive, take charge, set boundaries, and remain in control of our Energetic Intui-tive Body. Not only at the specific times that we are accessing our gifts, but also any time we are integrating the energy of those around us, and what we are absorbing from the collective.

From this place, we feel *more* confident and in tune with what we know to be true for us. We can make decisions based on the intuitive messages we're receiving without fear that we're being influenced by energy that's not our own. In this chapter, I will share how to harness the power of your own energy, along with tools and practical guidance for Energetic Self-Sovereignty. Remember, what works for one person might not work for you. This is about discovering what does, and becoming practiced at that.

IS THIS ENERGY MINE?

First of all, it's important to work out what energy is yours and what belongs to someone else. Including politicians, journalists, and the thousands of people you likely interact with on social media every day. There's a chance you've heard about "empaths," which is the term used to describe people who are more energetically sensitive—and if you're reading this book, chances are you fall somewhere on the empath spectrum. This can make it even easier to take on the emotions and physical symptoms of the people around you, without you even realizing it—a situation that can get very confusing. You may suddenly feel like there's something wrong with you, or experience a spike in anxiety that seems to come out of nowhere. If you're deeply connected to a person this can also happen across distances, as energy can be everywhere at once.

Even writing this chapter I took on the energy and physical symptoms of another person. I laughed after I realized what had happened. Writing away on a flight to Los Angeles, a mother and daughter seated next to me were communicating using sign language. I noticed this and carried on writing. As the flight progressed, my ears became more and more blocked with the cabin pressure, to the point that by the time we landed I was struggling to equalize my ears. Leaving the plane, I couldn't hear in my right ear, and it took a full 24 hours for my ears to clear. It was only then that I realized what had happened! Here I am writing about Energetic Self-Sovereignty, and ∞ gives me a physical experience to remind me how important it is.

One of the quickest ways to distinguish if the energy or emotions you're experiencing is yours is simply to ask: *"Is this energy mine?"* Here are some signs that you might be taking on energy that isn't yours.

IT'S SOMEBODY ELSE'S ENERGY WHEN ...

- It comes on quickly. You might suddenly feel anxiety, anger or fear that doesn't fit how you've been feeling. At the other end of the emotional spectrum, you might feel super hyper, excitable or playful. Please note that if you're around someone for a long time it can be a slow build as you take on more of their energy.
- You might feel pain, discomfort or body aches that don't quite fit your body. For example: *Why is my neck suddenly sore? Why do my teeth hurt? Why do I have pain in my feet?*
- You might feel drained or tired and want to retreat into your cave to not be around others because it feels "heavy" to be around them.
- You keep thinking about a person or a situation repeatedly and can't seem to shake it from your thoughts or energy sphere. You may even dream about them regularly.
- You just don't feel like yourself.

With time and practice you'll gain confidence as to how your own energy feels, and will be able to notice the signs of when another energy has entered your sphere. If you have more time, use the exercise below to get more clear.

BODY SCAN: IS THIS MY ENERGY?
Sit somewhere comfortable and close your eyes.

Scan your whole body, moving your awareness from your toes all the way up to the top of your head. See what you notice in terms of both your physical body and your emotional state.

If an emotion or physical symptom is present that doesn't feel like it belongs to you (use the signs shared above to help you) the next step is to ask, *"Who does this energy belong to?"* Trust the first thing that comes to you, whether it's a person, an organization, or even an article you read earlier on Facebook. You might not always get a clear hit, and that's okay. You can still release the energy even if you don't know exactly what or who is affecting you, the first step is simply to trust that something doesn't feel quite right.

Now, ask the energy to leave. You can do this in your head or say it out loud: *"I ask you to please leave my physical and energetic body."*

You can also "tap" the energy out of your body gently with your fingertips. Sit or lie down and tap your body slowly, with both hands and with gentle pressure. You can then increase the speed and the pressure if it feels good.

Allow yourself to be guided intuitively as to where you want to tap. But as a rule, if you're feeling an emotional symptom, gently tap the chest and heart space, and if you're feeling a physical symptom, tap the area that's being affected.

As you're tapping you can also say out loud or in your head: *"This is not mine. Please go."* Breathe into the area where you're tapping and you can even visualize a white light moving into this space to help you clear the energy.

When you intuitively feel that you're finished, stop tapping and gently rest the palms of your hands onto your body where you just tapped. Visualize the white light flowing with ease across your whole body. Finish by taking three deep breaths in through your nose and out of your mouth.

CONTROLLING THE INTUITIVE FLOW

It's also important to know that you don't have to be ON the whole time. There is yet more fear-based messaging in the New Age community implying that once you open up, ∞ gets to interact with you and your energy whenever they want. But this isn't the case. Having Energetic Self-Sovereignty also means you have the power to open your gifts up and shut them off, just like turning a light on and off. Of course, if ∞ wants to get your attention, they will. But it's not your job to drop everything and sit there with a neon "open" sign at your third eye 24/7.

To get the feel of how this works, try the two exercises below.

THE ENERGY FAUCET

Close your eyes, with your feet planted firmly on the floor, and begin by imagining water, or light, running out of a faucet. Now see this faucet positioned at the top of your head at your crown chakra. When you want to turn your gifts on you see the faucet being turned on and the water or energy beginning to flow over you.

Breathe in deeply, visualizing this energy flowing into your heart space. When you want to close up shop, visualize the faucet being turned off. Watch the water or energy slow its flow, and then stop completely. Take a few moments of stillness and reconnect with your breath by taking a series of deep, slow inhales and exhales.

NOT TODAY, THANK YOU

Another tip if you're being bombarded by messages from ∞, is to simply ask them to stop! Say it in your head or out loud: *"Not today thank you. I'm not available to connect right now. I see you. I acknowledge you. But I don't want to interact with you. Please leave."*

You can even swear and shout at them too if they don't get the message, and you can use this tool any time, anywhere. And please don't worry about making them "angry" or "upset." They understand and respect boundaries. It's not a "bad" thing to be firm, it's an important part of establishing Energetic Self-Sovereignty.

PSYCHIC ATTACKS ARE REAL ... HERE'S HOW TO DEAL

If you feel as if your energy is being negatively impacted on a more extreme level, you may be experiencing what's known as a "psychic attack." This happens when a negative energy enters your own energetic body with the malevolent intention of causing harm. This is different from simply experiencing somebody else's negative energy, and it will feel much more intense than the symptoms outlined above. It can make you feel and be physically sick, experience irrational reactions and mood swings, and as if there is a heavy cloud hanging over your head. Which sounds scary I know, but once this energy is cleared from your energetic body you'll be back to your "normal" energetic self.

I personally experienced a psychic attack in my early 20s, an experience that became my own biggest learning about the importance of Energetic Self-Sovereignty. I didn't know I had experienced it until after it happened. I was at a friend's 21st birthday party at her house in England—a house that was hundreds of years old, and steeped in history. We'd been drinking, and my friend's younger sister had taken us to visit a barn near the house which she'd turned into a den to make music. She offered us a joint and I had a small drag. I didn't smoke weed regularly but it was my friend's birthday and I thought, *"why not?"* As we were chatting I felt guided to ask: *"Why did you put the poster over there?"* She looked at me inquisitively and said, *"That's where his energy comes through, so I put it there to block him."* The second she said this I instantly felt a powerful, aggressively masculine energy leave the wall by the poster, enter my shoulder, and knock me over onto my side.

I lost my breath, and felt overwhelmed, as if there was something dark and heavy connected to me. The girls I was with were instantly concerned as they could see that something had happened to me. I described how the energy felt to them and the sister said that he had done this to her too.

Would it have happened if I hadn't been drinking and smoking? I don't think so. (I'll be talking in more detail about alcohol and other substances as they relate to your intuition later on in the book). It was as if the combination of the wine and the weed had left me wide open to this negative energy. I wasn't myself for a few days, even my Mum noticed the difference and asked if I was okay. I shared what had happened and with the help of my Mum and another professional healer they removed the negative energy from my body. They did this through a series of specific energy clearing tools and practices that they intuitively picked to work with this negative entity. It was a very stressful experience and something that I wouldn't wouldn't want to go through again, but it also made me realize just how sensitive and intuitive I am. It also gave me a newfound respect for caretaking my own energetic intuitive body, and was the catalyst for me learning tools and practices for how to ground and protect myself.

If you feel like you have experienced a psychic attack please go to a professional healer who specializes in negative entity removal. With a psychic attack you may need the support of someone else to help remove the energy. Choose a practitioner that you feel drawn to. In the Intuitive Action section I talk about how to pick aligned practitioners for you.

I share this story not to scare you, but because I know many of you reading will have had these experiences yourself. It's my mission to help you see your sensitivity as a superpower, instead of thinking of your gifts as a burden or in control of you. This story is here to empower you to develop Energetic Self-Sovereignty as a daily practice so you don't ever have to experience a targeted psychic attack. One of the quickest and most simple ways to do this is to make sure you are grounded and anchored into your energy. We can do this by using our own energy to create an energetic forcefield, as in the exercise below.

GROUNDING FORCE FIELD VISUALIZATION

I use this exercise before opening up to ∞, before a meditation, or any time I need to feel grounded before going to a social event or gathering. It's a quick and simple visualization that will help you feel confident and in charge of your energy.

Find a quiet space where you feel comfortable. Take off your shoes.

Sitting upright put your feet flat on the ground to connect into

Mother Earth like a plug.

Rest your hands on your lap or knees, palms facing either up or down. Choose what feels good.

Close your eyes. Imagine yourself surrounded by a forcefield of white light circling your whole body, including above your head, and underneath your toes. This forcefield represents your Energetic Self-Sovereignty and will only allow in what you want to call in.

Deepen your breathing, feeling the air you are taking in circulating throughout your entire body.

Now visualize the roots of a tree coming out of the bottoms of your feet and moving down into the center of the Earth. Imagine them moving through all the layers of earth and rock. Once these roots have reached the center of the Earth imagine them being tied into the earth for solid grounding.

Now imagine life force Earth energy (whatever this looks or feels like to you) coming back up the roots you just visualized and see it enter your body. Move this energy up your spine and into your whole body. Imagine this energy radiating out of your whole body like a forcefield that goes over your head, two feet away from your body and wraps under your feet.

If you feel called, you can also imagine yourself in a thick black cloak with a hood as you enter any space where you feel you may be more open to psychic attack. But do not use the cloak out of fear—it's only to be used when you feel it's really necessary.

ENERGETIC SELF-SOVEREIGNTY IN THE COLLECTIVE

Your energetic intuitive body is also part of the wider collective energy on this planet. It's what connects you to each and every other living person, animal, and element of the natural world. This is how you can physically feel love from another person, that deep connection when you're at your favorite spot in nature, or the camaraderie between supporters at a sports game. The emotional energy flows between us and is mirrored back to us so we feel it in our own energetic intuitive body.

This also means that when there's a lot going on at a societal level, it's easy for us to become overwhelmed. We feel uncertain, are easily triggered, and experience the underlying sense that we have no autonomy over our lives. The external chaos of the news cycle, of climate change, and social injustices, impacts our own sovereign energy field, and we begin to doubt and question our inner guidance system. However, with Energetic Self-Sovereignty the tables are turned. When we feel grounded in our truth, we begin to understand how great of an impact our *individual energy* can have on the collective.

Humans who chose to incarnate at the beginning of the 21st Century are living through very intense shifts on a planetary scale. Everything is changing, in terms of politics, globalization, social justice, the economy, and the environment. The sense of unease that this generates, sometimes veering into downright panic, impacts each of us on a deep energetic level, physically, emotionally and spiritually. Every time you turn on the news or open up your social media feeds, there is something new to take you energetically off balance. As a test, notice and name all the feelings you experience next time you scroll your social feed. You can use the exercise above to determine how much of this is really yours.

Some people in the spiritual community might say that the solution is just to stop giving negative events in the news more of our energy. But this is a form of spiritual bypassing. Our energy is part of the collective shift we wish to see for our planet and we have a responsibility NOT to consciously remove our energy. For change and transformation to take place we need to be informed, to stay engaged, and to understand fully what's taking place. This is the only way we can take aligned action to be part of the change.

Rather, the key lies in practicing discernment about the information we're receiving. But how do you navigate staying aware of what is happening but not taking it on energetically? This is where Energetic Self-Sovereignty comes in again. We have the power to regulate how we consume and interact with the negative events and the global media's response to it. Even if it's by only consuming news content for a set time limit or at a certain time in the day. Integrate the following tools into your life so you can create healthy energetic boundaries and strengthen your Energetic Self-Sovereignty.

PRACTICES FOR ENERGETIC SELF-SOVEREIGNTY

Set a time limit any time you're consuming the news media. Notice how it makes you feel, and turn it off when you know your capacity for absorbing new information has maxed out and it is beginning to leak into your energetic body. You may feel numb, emotionally overwhelmed, or like your breathing has become shallow or stopped altogether. It can feel like you are energetically "hooked in" to the energy, as if you've taken a drug.

Create space and time to process the energy of the collective. Delete a social media or news app for a few hours and practice the clearing and grounding practices above. You can also do the Energetic Clearing Guided Meditation that goes with this chapter.

Remember that you are in charge of the content you consume. If an account you're following drains your energy too much then give yourself permission to mute or unfollow them, even if it feels like you "should" keep following.

Get out in nature. Spending time with our primal energetic connection with Mother Earth away from the "noise" of technology and information can give your energy body a rest. If you live in a city you'll still receive the same effects by heading to your local park, however small it is. If you don't live near a green space you can bring nature into your home with plants and flowers.

If friends or family are continually sharing their fears with you, limit the time you're spending with them. Or, if you think they will be open to it, share some of what you have learned about Energetic Self-Sovereignty.

Stay vigilant as to when it feels like fear has become the predominant energy in your body. Ask yourself: *is this fear mine or is it the group fear of the collective?* Use the energy scan exercise above to "tap" the fear out of your body, and the Energy Faucet visualization to "turn off" the flow of fear into your body.

◇◇◇◇◇

INTUITIVE ACTION

Here are some more practical tools and techniques to support you with your Energetic Self- Sovereignty.

The Bubble Technique

If you're about to walk into a social or family gathering, work environment or concert venue to see your favorite band, call in the support of The Bubble. You can do it before you leave the house or in the car on your way there. Visualize yourself in a transparent bubble that goes over the top of your head, under your toes, and is as wide as your arm span. So you remain open to connecting with others, you can also imagine that this bubble has tiny holes in it. This means that you can put your energy out and receive the energy that feels good from others around you. When you get confident with this visualization you can just say the word "Bubble" in your head to call it quickly in.

Heart Center Preparation

Rub rose essential oil around your heart space to give your energetic emo-

ENERGETIC SELF-SOVEREIGNTY

tional body extra support. I like to do this before client sessions, meditations, meetings, or social gatherings. This is not about putting a protective blockade around the heart space, but giving it help feeling emotions and being open to vulnerability and learning.

You can also do a short version of the grounding energetic forcefield visualization, and simply rest your hands on your heart. Call in a green energy (the color associated with the heart chakra) and imagine this green light moving through your heart space preparing you to receive positive energy into the heart.

Aura Sprays and Energy Clearing Sprays

These are high vibrational natural sprays normally made from plant and flower essences or high grade essential oils. The energetic frequencies of the natural ingredients remove the lower vibrational energies and assist in clearing your energy.

You'll find plenty of versions for sale today, choose one that you feel intuitively drawn to energetically. I like to carry one when I travel, or am staying somewhere new. At big gatherings I carry a spray in my handbag and if I feel overwhelmed I nip to the bathroom to give myself a quick energy cleanse.

Talismans or Crystals

A talisman is a piece of jewelry you can wear to help guide you and keep your energy clear. It could be a necklace or a ring that holds special significance, and it might also contain a crystal. Sometimes this talisman will "find us"—we see it and we just know we're supposed to wear it. When a talisman has finished working to support you energetically, you may lose the piece, it may break, or you no longer feel the pull to wear it.

Some grounding crystals that can help you practice energetic self-sovereignty are Smoky Quartz, Fluorite, Obsidian, Shungite, Rose Quartz, and Jade. Crystals have different energetic vibrations which can assist us in regulating and clearing our own energy body. These crystals help to ground us by connecting us to the Earth's energy. Please always make sure your crystals are ethically sourced.

Energy Work, Body Work & Massage

Having the support of a practitioner you trust to clear your energetic body when needed is a powerful tool. Sometimes we can't clear all the energy on our own and need extra support—for example, if you've been experiencing a period when you've felt like you've been taking on lots of energy from others. You can find someone online or ask for a referral from someone in your community. But pick a practitioner that feels good to you. They can have all the qualifications, and a website full of great reviews, but if it doesn't feel like the right fit for you keep looking until it does. Energy work can also be done at a distance so you don't need to be in person for it to work. You just need to give them permission to enter your energetic intuitive body and they can do the energy clearing.

Salt

Salt is a powerful cleansing tool and is one of the quickest ways you can give your intuitive body a full energetic reset. Intuitives, witches, and healers have been working with it in their Energetic Self-Sovereignty practices for thousands of years. Regular weekly salt baths with Himalayan salt and baking soda will help to keep your energy body clear. You can use other salts, but the purer the salt the more powerful it will be. You can also take a shower with a salt bar and scrub your body. I sometimes like to gargle with salt water if I'm struggling to speak to my truth. You can also put salt at the entrance way to your home to help keep the energy clear. Or even under your bed in a small bowl for support while you sleep.

Self Led Energy Cord Retrieval

You can visualize yourself reclaiming your energy from others and removing other people's energy "cords." Energy cords connect the energy between people when you interact with them and are a normal, everyday occurrence—but sometimes it can help to consciously clear them. Find a quiet space. If there is someone you would like to have an energy reset from, imagine them standing in front of you. Notice in your body where you feel their energy cord attached to your energetic body. Now visualize the energy cord detaching from your body and going back to them. Let the person you are visualizing disappear and see yourself in your whole energy with no one attached to it. Breathe into your heart. Notice what emotions come up for you.

You can also use a crystal Selenite wand to "cut" energy cords from others, or from your phone or computer. Simply move the Selenite all over your body and visualize the cords being cut.

Orgasms & Self-Pleasure

Another great way to remove energy cords and practice Energetic Self-Sovereignty is through the power of orgasm and self-pleasure. Yes you read that right. You can do this to remove the energy of one person or the energy of the collective. Before you begin pleasuring yourself (and this can be done with a partner too), set the intention of the energy you wish to release. As you climax, imagine life force energy from the orgasm moving through your whole energetic intuitive body as it removes any cords attached to you. Pleasure and Energetic Self Sovereignty at the same time ... why not?

Washing Your Hands & Touching the Earth

A quick way to ground and clear your energy after being around people or to shut down your connection to your intuition is to touch the ground with both hands. This instantly grounds your energy back into the earth. If you have access to actual soil, then great, but you can also do this inside. Next, wash your hands, up to your elbows if you can, with soap and water. This will clear any residual energy.

Smoke Clearing

Also known as "smudging," clearing the energy in a space or your body with smoke is a traditional Indigenous practice. Traditionally this has been done with white sage, but with the rise in popularity of this technique we need to be aware of the sustainability of using this plant and the cultural appropriation attached to it. I will be explaining more about this in the Conscious Intuition Chapter coming up.

For something more conscious, buy or forage leaves from a plant that is native to your area, such as cedar, mugwort, rosemary, garden sage or thyme. Or grow it yourself. A cinnamon stick also works. First dry out the leaves, then burn some of the plant and move the smoke around your body or home to give it a reset. You do not need to light a whole bunch. One leaf is plenty.

Please note INTENTION is key for this practice. Without intention you're just waving smoke around—it will do nothing. To set an intention, say out loud or in your head that you will be using the smoke to clear any negative energies from your space or body. Imagine that there is white light coming from the smoke, clearing away anything negative, or any energy that belongs to others. When smoke clearing your body, start at your feet and work up to your head. Make sure you do the front and the back sides of your body. For a space, if there are windows and doors open them. Blow the smoke into the corners, cupboards and any other places you feel need clearing. Again, imagine that there is white light coming from the smoke. Move all the smoke out of the main doorway. Once you are done shut the windows and doors. After the main doorway is shut, blow the smoke around the door cracks from the inside. Repeat the mantra: "I shield myself, inside, outside, and within."

Sound & Movement

Playing music, dancing, moving your body, and singing work just as well as smoke clearing. The energetic sound frequencies of music and your voice shift lower vibrational energy from your space and energetic field. Ring bells and chimes around your home and over your body. Go to a sound bath. Do your favourite movement or exercise class. Your body *is* energy so when you move your body you are also resetting the energetic frequency and working with Energetic Self-Sovereignty. Again intention is important so say out loud or in your head that you wish to clear any negative energies from your space or body.

Essential Oils

As well as Rose (for the heart, above), Frankincense is a great oil for helping you feel centered and calm. I like to put this behind my ears or wherever I intuitively want it on my body. I also use Hinoki, Douglas Fir and other tree based essential oils for grounding support. For these oils I like to put them on the bottom of my feet. Tea Tree oil is my go to when I feel like I've taken on someone else's energy or I want to clear my own energy field. To do this, roll the oil onto the bottoms of your feet and down your spinal column from the top of your neck to the base of your spine. This will cut any energy cords from others.

GUIDED MEDITATION

The guided meditation for this chapter is an Energetic Clearing Guided Meditation. It's going to help you to ground and clear any energy cords attached to you. You can find it in the online portal.

REPEAT TO INVOKE ENERGETIC SELF- SOVEREIGNTY

I am in charge of my energy

I stand in my frequency

I am in the highest vibration of my truth

I have the power to allow aligned energy into my intuitive body

I can call on my energetic forcefield at will

And I have the power to clear the energy that is not mine

I am in charge of my energy

I stand in my energetic power

I hold the vision of my Energetic Self-Sovereignty

∞

4

TRUSTING YOUR TRUTH: AM I MAKING IT ALL UP?

It's the question I get asked the most: how do I trust what my intuition is telling me? How do I know it's real? Is it all my imagination? Is it my ego talking? *Am I making this all up?*

We've already discussed the extent to which we are conditioned by society not to trust our inner knowing, and to look outside of ourselves for guidance. We've all heard about trusting your gut, which is relevant, but it's more than just this. For this reason, developing the competency of trust, so that you know it is safe to pursue your truth and follow the guidance you are receiving, is paramount. Only from this place can you take action on the intuitive hits you're receiving. After all, the whole point is to be able to consciously use this skill in your everyday life, and align your thoughts and actions with what your intuitive body is trying to share with you.

Trust and intuition are deeply interconnected. Your intuition is like a muscle, and, ironically, the more you use it, the more you trust it. A dynamic that flows both ways, the more you learn to go with what you are receiving, the more guidance you will also be given, in a cyclical loop of self-empowerment. Leaning into this and feeling like you're *still* not "getting it" may be frustrating at first, the same as any time you're learning something new (even though, in this case, you're actually reactivating a skill you've always had access to). It can also feel risky, vulnerable, and a little unsafe.

It's natural to question your intuitive abilities. This may be when discouraging questions come up, such as: *How do I know if I'm acting on my in-*

tuition or if I'm acting out of fear? I made what I thought was an intuitive decision and I didn't get the outcome I had hoped for. Did I do it wrong? How do I know the difference between a real intuitive warning and my own fear talking? What if I'm just imagining the voice in my head, the subtle body tingles, or the fluttering of my heart? What happens if I want so badly to believe, I end up making stuff up?

Along with the deeply ingrained mistrust of our intuitive guidance, these fears also stem from us having been taught to act on what seems to be the most logical, rational, proven, or obvious thing to do. We learn this in childhood from our parents, caregivers, and in our school systems. It shows up in our approach to work and career, and how we make our money. This message is reinforced by the news cycle, and by political leaders and other people in positions of power. Remember, these are all part of a system that's *set up* to make you forget how to trust your intuition, and separate you from your own power. A system that was partly designed to keep us safe, but which often keeps us from living as the most liberated, empowered versions of ourselves—as this can make us a threat to existing power structures. For now, know that simply engaging with this book is part of a process of re-learning how to trust yourself. With your confidence in your inner truths restored, there is no limit to how powerful you can become.

By the end of this chapter you'll have an understanding of your personal blocks around trust, and where this is holding you back from using your intuition to live a life that's fully aligned with your truth. I'm also going to teach you the difference between egoic, fear based thoughts (which might seem like intuitive messages at first), and the genuine, intuitive insights that you have access to 24/7.

WHY IT'S SO HARD TO TRUST

First of all, it's important to acknowledge that we all have issues trusting ourselves to a degree. This is a result of societal programming that asks us to trust external power figures over ourselves, and it can also be shaped by our childhood and adult relationships. Getting to the root of our inability to trust ourselves is key to moving beyond this into a state of intuitive alignment, and this means first dropping down into what's known as our shadow self. It is here that we often find what's blocking us from trusting our inner truth and power. Not to mention making it hard for us to trust in romantic relationships, in our business partnerships, in our relationship with money, and even in our wider community. We question, will the relationship last? Will they let us down? Will they be honest with us? Looking at our current world leaders, it's also increasingly clear that most are more invested in their own interests than in doing what's right for the people.

Navigating these shadow trust issues is all part of the dance between the subconscious ego patterning that really just wants to keep us safe, and the ways we then self-sabotage by blocking ourselves from living from our intuition. This is why identifying these blocks is such a game changer. Have a look at the questions below and answer as honestly as you can:

In what areas do you struggle with trust? (love, work, money?)
To what extent do you trust your own beliefs, thoughts and feelings?
To what extent do you trust others in what they say and do?
To what extent do you trust others to support you emotionally?
To what extent do you trust that you are following the right path in life?

The brief visualization practice below will give you further clarity. If anything in the exercise brings up emotions you feel uncomfortable with, remember, you are in charge. You can open your eyes and come out of it at any time.

VISUALIZATION FOR TRUST

Sit somewhere with your feet flat on the floor to ground you.

Close your eyes.

Connect with your breath, and take several deep breaths into your belly and out of your mouth.

Visualize the word TRUST in your mind.

Now move the word so you can feel it in your body. How does it feel in your body?

What emotions are present? Where do you feel them in your body? Allow your mind to wander and notice any particular memories that come up for you around trust.

Don't force anything to appear, simply allow anything connected to trust to show itself to you.

If nothing comes up for you, that's okay. Trust that.

If a memory comes up, notice the emotions that are present.

Sit in this space for as long as you need.

When you're ready, reconnect to your deep, belly breaths.

Wiggle your hands and your toes. Slowly open your eyes and come back into the room.

After you finish the visualization, make a note of anything that came up for you. What memories came up? What did you feel? Go slowly with this. If you are feeling emotional or sensitive and can't get the words out, pause and let what came up rise to the surface. *Your body knows what to do with whatever came up.*

Allow this exercise to be the beginning of a process for you to un-cover the root of your issues with trust. The next step is to do a release of these blocks. When we perform a release ritual it ener-getically clears them as part of your wider healing journey.

To do this, take what you wrote down after the visualization, and read it out loud. Speaking your truth in this way acknowledges the blocks you have around trust. So often we don't get to "hear" our emotions out loud, and externalizing them like this is a way to pro-cess them out of our bodies.

The next step is to burn what you've written while speaking the following incantation:

I release my fears around trust
I release what makes me fearful

I release [say out loud anything personal to YOU that came up from
the visualization]

I am ready to develop my relationship with trust

I am open to trust

I trust myself

I trust

You can also use the "I Trust Myself" guided meditation that goes
with this chapter. More information on this can be found in the Intuitive Action section.

YOUR INTUITION DOESN'T ALWAYS TALK SENSE

Our trust issues make even more sense considering that what we're hearing often ... won't. This is because the intuitive voice doesn't always follow
"logic." When something illogical emerges from your energetic intuitive
body, the first thing your rational mind wants to do is either make sense
of it or discount it. "Why would you do it that way?" it wants to know.
Then comes the cautionary "advice": "I wouldn't if I were you, you might
get hurt / mess up / be laughed at." But like that team building exercise
where you have to fall backwards into a group of people, and trust that
they're going to catch you, now is the time to take a leap and lead with
your intuition.

After all, since when did magic, inspiration, and creativity have anything to do with logic? The intuitive brain and the rational brain are two
completely separate operating systems. The rational brain needs facts
and proof, and operates within safety limits and specific timeframes.
Meanwhile, the intuitive mind runs on creativity, imagination, noticing,
feelings, and is surrendered to time taking its own time. In our fast-paced,
competitive world, the logical mind reigns supreme because we want
quick answers, instant gratification, and feel it's "safer" to listen to it. But
intuition is anything *but* logical.

To the extent that even when we've learned to trust and act on our
intuition, the message will still often only make sense *after* the event. After

all, it's only after you've chosen to trust your inner guidance over your rational mind, have acted on it, and are able to look back and reflect on what happened, that you can see what was unfolding all along.

Perhaps you feel called to take a different route home, and you find out later that there was a big accident the way you normally go. In a more impactful example, you may find yourself on a date with somebody who's exactly your type on paper ... but something about their energy doesn't feel right. If you have any fears about not being able to find a partner, it may seem logical to override this inner knowing and try to "make it work." Before you know it, you've wasted months, if not years, in a relationship that was never meant for you.

But please, no beating yourself up for all the times you didn't listen to your intuition. We have all, myself included, found ourselves in messy situations, looking back and asking: "Why didn't I listen to my instincts? I knew what to do all along!"

Given how little we've been taught about how to work with our inner guidance, it's likely you actually had no idea your intuition was trying to get your attention in the moment. It's only with hindsight you can see what was going on. Even having made this my life's work, it is an ongoing journey to form a deeper daily bond with my own intuition. Growing up, I stayed friends with certain people even though part of me knew they couldn't be trusted and didn't have my best interests at heart.

In my previous career, I remember getting the hit that I was going to lose a job. I kept pushing it aside, until four days later I was let go. There have been times when I've taken on a client I knew wasn't a good fit, and it's turned into a tricky situation. Or I'll be cooking at home, and the voice in my head goes, "Hey, be careful, you might burn yourself!" And then five seconds later, I'm running my hand under the cold tap watching a blister bubble up.

In the above instances, there was little I could do to prevent being fired or burning my hand. But in the case of choosing who to open up to as a friend, or commit to a working relationship with, learning to trust my intuition could have saved me so much trouble and helped me stay in my Energetic Self-Sovereignty.

Reflect back on your life and write down some key moments where you got an intuitive hit on something but you didn't act on it.

What stopped you from trusting your inner knowing?

What were the consequences of you not listening?

How might things have gone differently if you'd been able to trust your intuition?

IS IT MY EGO, IS IT FEAR, OR IS IT MY INTUITION?

Learning to differentiate between the different voices in your head is often the key missing piece when it comes to trusting your intuition, as it will help you tune into and prioritize what it's telling you. The thing is, all these voices sound *just like you*. Let's take a closer look at the role of these three inner voices.

Your ego is the voice of your external identity, or how you see yourself in the world. It is also the part of you that keeps up a running commentary of the fears, worries, desires, needs and judgments you generate daily just by being a human in the world. If it gets to yammer on totally unchecked, this can make you feel overwhelmed, as if you're drowning in your thoughts. It can also begin to hijack your body, making you feel anxious, nauseous, angry, or frustrated. When this chatter is running the show, it's very hard to hear the softer, gentler voice of your intuition.

It's easy to see why common wisdom in the New Age community is that the ego is a "negative" part of us, and that we should do our best to try to transcend it. And it's true that paying it too much attention can be the cause of so much suffering. But if we truly lived from a place of no ego, we'd be denying the fact that we're still humans having a human experience on this planet. Not to mention that when we suppress our fears, desires and the emotions connected to them, it ultimately causes us more pain and suffering. It's actually when we accept the duality that lies within us, no longer viewing the ego and its concerns as either good or bad but simply a part of our whole self, that we truly step into our authentic truth and power.

This can also be said for the Fear Voice, which is the voice of our inner survival instinct. We are all programmed with a fight, flight, or freeze mechanism to help us respond to danger. The Fear Voice is the Ego Voice with the volume turned up, and it kicks in during times of panic and acute stress and discomfort. Although this mind is programmed within us to help us survive in these moments, more often than not, it can be hard to distinguish between what is real and our Fear mind causing even more chaos as we lose all perspective. This is why discovering how to use and trust your Intuitive Voice during these times is a skill to relearn and master.

Meanwhile, your Intuitive Voice is here to support you and guide you. It's important to stress again that all these voices will "sound" like *you*. You're not going to suddenly hear strange voices from another realm or the "voice of God" in your head. But unlike the Ego / Fear Voice, which is like your personal trainer barking at you, your Intuitive Voice will sound confident, gentle, and calm. You'll also hear it from the "back" of your head, while the Ego / Fear Voice will come from the "front" of your mind. The Intuitive Voice also isn't hungup on things happening on any particular time frame, or on any specific outcome. This can make it feel riskier to trust, as nine times out of ten we want the Intuitive Voice to show up when we need an answer quickly! What actually happens, is that your Intuitive Voice will deliver its message and then disappear —the skill being learning to listen *when it speaks to you*, versus trying to make it show up *when you want*. The Ego / Fear Voice on the other hand, is ever-present, chattering away in your head and urging you to act NOW.

This is actually a key way you can distinguish between an Ego / Fear based message and your intuitive guidance. Notice: what message has been playing on a loop in your head the past day or so? What would happen if you just let the need to act on this go, and trusted that the "real" time and course of action to pursue will simply let itself be known?

Now let's look at some other ways to tell the difference between ego, fear, and intuition.

QUALITIES OF THE EGO VOICE

- You can't stop thinking about something and the voice keeps going round and round in your head. *Am I doing enough? Should I do something different? Is this going to work?*

- The voice has an agenda, expectation, goal, or plan. *When am I going to get that job? I need to know if they're the one. My five year plan says I should be doing this by now.*

- There is a desire for a logical and obvious "solution" to fix a situation or get guidance. *I must work out a detailed, step-by-step plan for how to proceed and make changes in my life.*

- It wants an answer NOW! *I should have worked this out by now! I don't have time to wait! I have a deadline to make a decision.*

- The Ego Voice often uses the words "should," "would," or "must." *I should do it this way. I must act now. How would that be perceived?*

Location
The Ego Voice comes from the front of the head.

In the Body
Can make your body feel tense or tight.

Quality of Voice
Chattering
Fast paced
Fearful
Foggy
Easily led

Emotional Guide
Anxiety

Panic

Confidence

Motivation

Overwhelm

Confusion

Frustration

Anger

QUALITIES OF THE FEAR VOICE

- Wants to control everything around them including the actions and emotions of others. *The more control I have the "safer" I will be.*

- Suspicious and paranoid. *Wants to question everything and everyone, including yourself.*

- Kicks in during stressful events, conversations, relationships, uncertainty or trauma. *It's time to get into survival and protection mode.*

- Fear of the unknown, uncertainty, and not knowing. *What might happen to me? I don't have a plan. What will this mean for the future?*

- Feels like it's missing out on something. *I might miss out on that opportunity. I don't want to fail at any cost. I want to feel differently from how I am feeling right now.*

Location, Emotional Guide, and Quality of Voice

Just like the Ego Voice it comes from the front of the head. It will have the same voice quality and emotional guide as the Ego Voice, but amped up—like having a military general barking orders at you or the volume dial being turned up to MAX. When the Ego Voice has got your attention, it can feel impossible to ignore what it is telling you. Your whole enegrgtic intuitive body feels like it's on overdrive, and everything seems overwhelming, chaotic, and out of control.

QUALITIES OF THE INTUITIVE VOICE

- Guidance comes in and then disappears from your mind. *Speak to this person. Listen to this creative idea. Do this. Go there. Take action. You will hear it once and it won't keep niggling at you.*

- Isn't attached to any desire or outcome. *Nothing is "right" or "wrong," and it doesn't matter what I think I "want."*

- Doesn't feel forced or have an agenda. *I surrender up energetically to what is happening or will happen in the future.*

- Feels good in your body and energetic sphere. *Something just feels "right" as if I know it to be true.*

- Doesn't feel fixed or logical but you want to know more. *May offer up a different path or route that you had not thought of. What about doing it this way?*

- Timing is flexible or does not factor at all. *It doesn't matter when it happens, my job is to stay on the path and trust where I am being taken.*

- Feels like it wants to support you and guide you. *Feels like a best friend or confidante that always wants the best for you. Feels like it has your back and wants you to succeed.*

Location

Deep in the back of the head or mind.

In the Body

May be felt throughout your whole intuitive body, as body tingles, warmth, cold breeze
(There's a whole chapter coming up on how you can identify the bodily sensations of your Intuitive Voice)

Quality of Voice

Confident
Calm
Rational
Trustworthy
Guiding

Emotional Guide
Calm
Centred
Balanced
Peaceful
Reassured

BEING OKAY WITH NOT KNOWING

Nobody can ever know everything. It doesn't matter how strong your gifts are, you're never going to be able to use your intuition to become an all seeing, all knowing being. Part of the beauty of our human experience is *not knowing* and being in your intuitive power means practicing the art of surrender and letting go of control.

Which is easier said than done. We would prefer to try and control all aspects of what is happening in our lives, as this creates the illusion of safety. Which is why developing and trusting your Intuitive Voice is imperative.

When we become too fixated on wanting to know everything, including what's coming up for us in the future, the Ego / Fear Voice mind can take over. But this only leads to more panic and fear. So when your Intuitive Voice comes in and gives you the guidance, it is key for you to practice surrender to the outcomes.

Mastering surrender is not an overnight process, and even when you think you've got it dialed in you'll find yourself being tested again. But it is when we realize that we can't be a master puppeteer in our lives, and that all we can do is deal with what is happening in the NOW, that we reclaim our agency and power.

WHAT AM I TRYING TO CONTROL?

Scan your life right now and get honest with yourself on what you're trying to control.

Are you trying to control a relationship?

Are you trying to control the timing of something?

Are you trying to control an outcome to what you want it to be?

Are you trying to control your reactions/emotions?

Now look at the below list, which shifts the energy to a practice of surrender.

I surrender trying to control this [enter the person/relationship]

I surrender the timing of [enter what you're controlling]

I surrender the outcome of [enter what situation you're controlling]

I surrender feeling [enter your feelings/emotions you're controlling]

Can you see how surrender energetically opens you up to receive intuitive guidance in these areas of your life? By starting a practice of surrender you're letting the ego know that it has nothing to fear. That you're "okay" with any outcome. Learn to flip into surrender mode any time you feel like you're becoming too controlling.

WAIT, IS THIS A WARNING?

As well as helping us find a YES that is aligned with who we truly are, our intuition can also help when it comes to red flags or warnings about what NOT to do. This can simply show up as the feeling that something bad might happen. Some people experience what they might think are prophetic dreams, or omens. However, these warnings can also be hard to trust when they get mixed up with fear. For example, you might find yourself thinking, "I have a feeling that X person doesn't like me. Do I hang out with them?" Or, "I'm worried the plane might crash. Do I go on that trip?"

This confusion can be heightened when there are big events in the news, or when we're facing issues as a collective that can impact our Energetic Self-Sovereignty (as discussed in Chapter 3). In these situations, the collective energy can also impact our ability to trust ourselves and our truth, and to own our intuitive power. We can get pulled this way and that, unsure what to believe, what point of view to take, or how we should respond. We may find ourselves going along with the mass response, even though it doesn't align with who we are and what we believe inside. On both an individual and a collective level, cultivating and developing the ability to separate the red flags from the red herrings is vital.

Here's an exercise to help you work out what's a genuine intuitive warning, and what's just fear based noise.

- Were you already feeling scared or fearful before you got the "warning"?
- Is the energy in the collective heightened, due to what's happening with global events?
- If you answer "yes" to either of the above, name exactly what you're feeling scared or worried about. Either say it out loud, write it down, or simply acknowledge it.
- Now refer back to the section above on how to distinguish between your Ego / Fear Voice, and your Intuitive Voice. Which voice is delivering this warning? Be honest with yourself. Don't try and make it fit the qualities of your intuition.
- If the warning genuinely carries the energies of your intuition, then trust the message you're receiving, and whatever action feels good for you. If it fits more than one of the Ego / Fear qualities, don't rush into anything. Pause, watch, and wait.
- If the Intuitive Voice is clear and is asking you to act on something "now"—take action!

As mentioned, one quality of a warning from the Ego / Fear mind is that you can't stop thinking about it. The voice or warning keeps going 'round and 'round in your mind. Meanwhile, an intuitive red flag will come in swiftly, deliver the message, and then disappear from your mind. This makes it easier to "miss" the intuitive warning, especially if you are already feeling panicked or stressed, so it's vital to try to slow down any time you find yourself in a place of fear or anxiety. This might feel counterintuitive when you're trying to act fast on a warning—but all you need to remember is to pause and connect to your breath. You can also practice the Energetic Self-Sovereignty tools on page 56 to support you. Please always trust that you will receive an intuitive warning when you need to hear it.

∞∞∞

INTUITIVE ACTION

As you are learning by now, working with your intuition takes time and practice, as with developing any skill. The same goes with learning to trust your intuitive messages. Here are some simple exercises you can use to strengthen this part of the process. Use them any time you're unsure about taking action on intuitive guidance you've received or if you're questioning a warning and want to know if it's real.

Breathe into the Intuitive Heart

The intuitive heart is a powerful place of intuition. Use this short exercise to access it:

Close your eyes. Take a few deep breaths in through the nose and out through the mouth to settle your energy and connect you to your energetic intuitive body.

Visualize either the question you want an answer to, the intuitive message you've received, or the warning you want more clarity on. Picture it any way that feels right and see it surrounded by white light.

When you feel ready, visualize a green energy around it, and then breathe the question or message all the way into your heart space.

Now ask yourself: how does this feel in my heart space?

A "yes" or a positive response may feel like a slight buzzing, fluttering, or energetic expansion of the heart space or across your whole body.

A "no" may just feel like a no, or you might feel a heaviness in your heart, coldness, or a feeling of restriction in your heart or across your whole body.

Trust what you are getting and go with the first feeling that comes up. Trust it, even if the answer doesn't make logical sense. This is part of exercising your intuitive muscle. The more you trust, the more intuitive guidance you will receive.

Boost your Solar Plexus
The energy center or chakra associated with trust is the Solar Plexus, which sits roughly an inch above your belly button. The color associated with this energy point is yellow, and you can rebalance and boost the energy of the Solar Plexus to strengthen your ability to trust. Here's how:

Close your eyes and sit somewhere comfortable.

Start by doing the grounding forcefield visualization from Chapter 3.

Once you have completed this, imagine a small glowing disc of energy in the area of your Solar Plexus. Visualize it getting bigger.

Now see the disc spinning one way and then the other. Imagine it clearing out any stuck or imbalanced energy in this power center.

Repeat this as often as you feel called.

∞∞∞

GUIDED MEDITATION

Access the Guided Meditation for Trust on the online portal. I created this meditation specifically to help you release your fears around trusting and to support you in calling in the energy of trusting in the unknown.

REPEAT TO INVOKE TRUST

I open myself up to my Intuitive Voice and I trust its guidance

I trust that I am always being guided into my truth

I trust that ∞ is supporting me on my life journey

I trust my energetic intuitive body

I trust my intuitive heart

I am ready to take action on what I know is my truth

I am open to trust

I trust myself

I trust

∞

5

NOTICING & THE POWER OF IMAGINATION

By now you should be getting more comfortable with the fact that *you are intuitive!* Hopefully you're feeling less fearful about using your gifts, and have been able to see how and why you may have been blocking yourself from accessing your intuition. Chances are this also means you've started listening out for intuitive messages and guidance ... and that you may also be sitting there, thinking: *"why am I still not getting anything?!"* If this is the case, it's probably because you're simply not *noticing* the messages that are coming through for you.

The majority of us move through life in our own individual worlds, to the extent that we don't really notice the subtle nuances and small details of the wider world around us. This means we also miss the signs, symbols and messages that we are receiving into our energetic intuitive body constantly. We're busy rushing from A to B, working through our to-do lists and focussing on our goals for the future. In our downtime, our attention is absorbed by our phones, by the latest addictive series on TV, or by trawling news and shopping sites on the internet.

But underneath all this busyness and noise, the truth is we are all receiving intuitive guidance all the time. All the while we're on our laptops, working out, in the shower, walking the dog, chilling at home, and out with friends, our intuitive body is receiving and delivering information to help guide us as we move throughout our day. This guidance exists right here, right now, not way out on some alternative dimension of reality, which means all you need to be able to access it is to start *noticing*.

This means paying closer attention to your surroundings, to your emotions and, on a deeper level, to the themes that keep playing on repeat in your life. But in a world where we're expected to constantly be doing, consuming, and achieving, this is another skill that must be re-learned. It also means facing our collective fear of slowing down. We fear slowing down because we've been conditioned that we might miss out on something. That we might not achieve success, that we'll miss an opportunity, or that we won't be included socially. Subconsciously we can also fear slowing down because we worry what will come up for us if we do. When we're busy it's easier to block out the emotions we don't want to feel, the situations we don't want to face, or to ignore how our heart is truly asking us to live our lives. We can only begin to notice our guidance when our emotional, physical and spiritual body isn't being overwhelmed with all the information created by our need to "do." Our intuition relies on us allowing it space so we can receive it, notice it, process it, and decode its guidance.

The truth is that this guidance is around us and within us everyday. Not just in nature, but in our homes, our towns and cities. When we begin to notice this, we begin to see everything with wonder. We take in the richness of the colors, textures, and materials of our day-to-day reality. Noticing also allows you to feel connected to others, presenting us with an opportunity to actually "see" the people around us versus simply knowing there's another human in your proximity. On the inside we can start to notice our feelings, and actually take time to enjoy the sensation of love, gratitude and joy in our lives. And on the flipside, noticing is also a powerful way to connect to the underbelly of our own lives, and the hidden, often uncomfortable truths of our communities and our collective world. Where before we may have been willing to turn a blind eye, noticing gives us insight into what we need to heal as a collective.

The second piece of this intuitive puzzle is learning how to combine this noticing with the creative power of our *imagination*—another innate skill we all possess, but which tends to get written off as childish and unrealistic, reserved for fairy tales and kids' playground games. But when we learn to work with our imagination as adults it becomes an integral part of hearing our inner guidance, discovering the meaning of our emotions, and accessing the space of our intuition. Let me show you how.

SLOW DOWN TO CREATE SPACE

The first step to becoming re-skilled in the art of noticing and imagination, is to step out of the societal conditioning of "doing" and into an energy of *being*. This means slowing down and taking our time with life, which frees up space in our day to notice and use our imagination. This becomes a two-way street; as we practice the art of noticing we are also fortifying our ability to stay present, calm, aware and connected to our body, which is the tool through which we receive intuitive guidance. As we get out of our heads and begin to quiet the chatter of the Ego / Fear Voice (which is also the voice that's constantly pushing us to do and achieve more) something magical happens:

We notice how we're feeling.
We notice what doesn't feel right.
We notice what we've been avoiding.
We notice what we're holding in our bodies.
We notice what makes us shut down and what makes us come alive.

Simply put, we detach from what we "think" we should be doing or feeling, and drop into the sensation and the knowings that are guiding us towards our truth. We become more aware of not only the signs and messages in our exterior world, but also the information that's stored in our emotional, physical and spiritual body.

The thing is, many of us don't want to slow down out of fear of what might come up. We resist creating internal space because we don't *want* to notice what's trying to get our attention. This is because part of us knows that slowing down will also mean looking at all the untruths we've been living. Will mean peering into our shadowy blind spots. May mean a painful shattering of any illusions we have been laboring under, forcing us to make some big changes in our lives. And so we avoid it at all costs. We pile on the tasks and the goals, focusing on manifesting more and more, to ensure that we're kept busy. We may also focus on helping others, or the issues of the wider world, so we don't have to look at what's actually happening for us. But when we resist slowing down and dropping into this place of pause, we are stepping out of our inner truth and staying disconnected from our power. By not allowing ourselves to be authentic we also cut ourselves off from our intuition.

If you think this might be you, please don't think you've done anything wrong. It can be painful, confusing, and deeply uncomfortable to be with the whole truth of our inner selves. Layered on top of this, there are forces at work in the world that benefit from our collective numbness and amnesia, which don't want us to look at the truths of our planet and of the collective. And so we have been conditioned by the colonialist patriarchy to keep going, to not stop, to focus on tasks and personal successes, so we don't have time to see the truths of greed, inequality, and oppression in our society. By busying ourselves with our everyday lives, we actually get to ignore the suffering of others. But when we slow down, take a pause, and rest for just a moment, everything we've been avoiding comes up to the surface. We will never be able to unsee what we now know, and as overwhelming as this might seem, this is also where we find our opportunity to be part of the collective change—as we are reconnected to our inner power.

WHAT ARE YOU AVOIDING?

Read through the below questions to see if you're in a space of noticing or a space of avoidance:

Do you spend most of your day thinking about the next thing you need to do?

Do you often feel like you're rushing from A to B?

Does your thinking often feel scattered?

Does the thought of doing nothing bring up anxiety or fear?

Do you often help others to the point that you feel burnt out?

Do you compartmentalize your emotions because you think they will slow you down?

Are you avoiding people or conversations so you don't have to deal with something?

If you answered "yes" to two or more of these questions, it's time to create some space so you can re-activate the skills of noticing and imagination and take back your power.

WAYS TO GET INTO A SPACE OF NOTICING
Create more space in your diary. Make sure you add in breaks throughout the week. Try not to book things back to back so you feel rushed or overwhelmed.

Create space in your life by saying "no." Saying no doesn't make you a bad person, it simply creates boundaries to what isn't energetically aligned for you. Which in turn means you are in your authentic truth and in your power.

Schedule in "you" time during the week like you would anything else in your diary. Even if it's just taking 15 minutes to go for a walk on your own, take a bath, read your favorite book, or do something else you love. You can even block it off in your diary if you think this will help you.

Have a morning and evening routine that gives you time to not feel rushed. Set your alarm a little earlier. Take 10 minutes to meditate in the morning and before bed.

Journal. Writing may feel like another "to-do" but when you give yourself permission to simply journal on whatever comes up it can be a great way to connect to your emotions. It doesn't have to be long, you can just write down one word that sums up your day.

Conscious walking and driving. As you move about your day, ask: do you need to walk or or drive so fast? Or are you going at that speed because you're rushing to get to the next "thing"?

Write down what you feel like you're avoiding in your life. Use this list to get really real with yourself about what you've been suppressing with busyness and what is ready to be felt. Don't feel like you have to do this alone. Call on the help of a counselor, therapist or support worker if needed.

YOUR CREATIVE IMAGINATION

Slowing down also allows us to connect to our creative imagination. Our imagination is an aspect of a universal creative energy flow that we all have access to, as well as a key component of our energetic intuitive body. When we connect with it and step into its flow we can use its energy to help guide us intuitively. Noticing helps us do this; by allowing ourselves to slip into a state of noticing, we also allow the subconscious visions and inspirations of our creative imagination to come to the surface. This gives us access to our unique inner resourcefulness, and to our most innovative ideas, visions and passions. All of which show us ways we can express our intuitive power in the world. Using your imagination is not about "making things up," "wishful thinking," or seeing "hallucinations." It is another vital part of how we connect to our wisdom and our truth, and of using our intuitive gifts to guide us in our everyday life.

We are all born with the skill of imagination. Even if you don't think of yourself as a particularly "creative" person, or as someone who gets to use their imagination on a regular basis, this part of you is constantly active. As children we are naturally very connected to this part of ourselves, making up games and stories and letting our imagination run free. We allow ourselves to daydream and let our mind wander where it wants to go. We don't put limits on the possibilities it's showing us or try to control the outcome. We just go with it. But as we get older, we absorb the conditioning that imagination is just for "play" and isn't something we can apply to our work and goals in the "real world." Over time, we turn the volume on this part of our inner world down, until we can no longer hear it.

Earlier I spoke about how this can be a block to connecting to our gifts, as it can bring up inner doubts and fears as you question: "Am I making this stuff up? Is this my intuition or my imagination?" Accessing your imagination, and then TRUSTING it, is part of connecting to your intuitive power. This is why learning to get back into the space of creative imagination is extremely important. It starts by slowing down, noticing what's present, and creating inner space for your imagination to flourish. A simple way to access and develop your imagination is to visualize and recall memories from the past. Let's try it out.

SPECIAL PLACE IMAGINATION VISUALIZATION

Find somewhere to sit where you feel comfortable and safe and gently close your eyes.

Imagine you're standing outside a childhood home, building or space that you have happy memories of or feel connected to.

Next imagine you're at the front door or entranceway. What does it look like? What color is the door? Is there a door handle? Is the door slightly ajar?

Now enter the building, space, or room.

Visualize yourself in the surroundings. What can you see? How does it make you feel?

Imagine yourself walking through the building, space or home to your favorite part of the space you're in.

Imagine you are there right now. What can you see? What can you smell? Is there anyone with you?

Take some time to notice all the details. How is the room decorated? Are there windows? What can you see outside?

Now go a little deeper: How does it make you feel to be here? What memories are being brought up for you?

When you are ready to leave this space, slowly wiggle your hands and your toes. Take a few deep belly breaths and open your eyes.

If you feel called, take some extra time to journal on anything that came back for you during this visualization. You can also practice by going to revisit other places or memories that you would like to recall.

MAGIC IS ALL AROUND YOU

When was the last time you walked into a space or spent time outside, and really took in all the details? Took time to notice the colors, textures, sounds, smells, words, or imagery, in the world around you. Without thinking about it, if you were to close your eyes right now in the space where you're reading this book, would you be able to describe in detail the layout of the room, everything that's in it, and all the small details of your environment?

One of my favorite things to do is to go for a walk without my phone and just notice what's around me. Or I'll go for a drive with the stereo off and let the silence be the backdrop to what I am observing. In these activities I will usually receive some form of intuitive message that helps me that day. If I'm feeling a bit off I might notice somebody wearing a T-shirt that says "SMILE." And I remember to smile. I might be feeling stuck looking for life direction, and a new perspective appears out of a situation in a movie or on TV. Or I'll hear a song while I'm out and about and it feels like the lyrics are talking to me. I also love to notice who pops into my thoughts when I'm in this space. When that happens I'll reach out to them—or more often than not, they'll reply saying, *"I was just thinking about you!"* All these are examples of intuitive messages, but you will never experience them until you take the time to notice them.

When you notice these messages, the next step is to access your creative imagination to discover what they mean for you. To do this you can visualize or imagine yourself connected to what you've noticed, felt or experienced. For example, once you've seen the T-shirt that says "SMILE" you then imagine seeing someone smiling. Notice the details and see a close up of teeth and upturned lips. You might even imagine what it feels like to smile in your energetic body. You can also go one step further and ask yourself: why am I being reminded to smile today? These steps connect you to the channel of your creative imagination as well as the positive energy of smiling, which in turn may actually make you smile! And in that moment, your energy shifts, and you experience a simple moment of joy.

The intuitive guidance you're receiving doesn't always have to be *life changing*. Subtle intuitive messages like the one described above can be just as empowering and helpful as we go about our day. But perhaps, in the magic of noticing, you will also receive a special lightbulb idea or sudden clarity about a situation that previously felt like a dead end. Using our intuitive gifts isn't just about predicting the future or making big decisons; it is a way to connect more deeply to the present moment in the here and now.

NOTICING NUMBERS

As you begin to work with your intuition, you might begin to notice repetitive numbers like 111, 222, 333, 444, 555, etc. Or other numbered sequence patterns that have a special relevance to you. It can be confusing when you start to see them and you might wonder why they're showing up. The traditional New Age spiritual labeling for these number patterns is "angel numbers." As if these supernatural beings are trying to give you messages.

There's a lot of conflicting information in online articles and dedicated books on how you should interpret these signs. But before reading any external definition, always ask yourself: why do *I* think these numbers are showing up? What do they mean *for me*? I'll be sharing more about how to do this in the chapter on decoding messages that's coming up next.

When I ask what seeing numbers means for me, I simply get a reminder that our intuitive energy is connected to what we experience in our outside world. I see repeating numbers simply as a visual sign that we are all part of an energetic matrix, and as a reminder that everything is connected and that we are all part of the collective energy.

You may also notice that people who become obsessed with seeing numbers come to energetically rely on them as a way to feel they're on the "right" path. Notice if you're falling into this trap by always looking out for numbers on buildings, clocks, and number plates. Remember, being connected to your intuitive power and trusting in your unique path is not based on seeing number patterns. If anything, let them be a nice visual energy boost, versus a crutch to live your life by.

NOTICING PATTERNS AND THEMES

Once you slow down, create space and start noticing, you will likely begin to see the themes and patterns that are interwoven with the fabric of your life. For example you're thinking of ending things with a partner, quitting a job, or calling time on a friendship, and the theme of "letting go" and "new beginnings" seems to be following you around. Or you're struggling with making a life decision and themes around "trust" or "it's ok to take your time" appear. These repeating messages may show up externally in your conversations and in what you're reading or listening to. They may also appear in your dreams, and in the people, ideas, and creations that you feel drawn to. The repetition of these themes in themselves are messages for you.

For example, as I was writing this chapter I had multiple conversations over the span of a week where "out of the blue" people would start talking about or mentioning spiders! My mum started singing the nursery rhyme "incy wincy spider." Talking to my sister on FaceTime, she said she thought she saw a spider on my hand. A friend brought up the notion of spiders being connected to the feminine principle. A client in Australia emailed about spiders in her house. I even had a "random" conversation with an Uber driver who was also a professional storyteller. We chatted and he began to tell me a folktale from Africa ... about a spider. To cap it off, I then found a real spider in my bathtub—the first time I've seen one in the year I've lived in my current apartment.

By which point I was like, "OK I'M NOTICING! What's the intuitive message for me in this? Why does this theme keep showing up in my life?" To interpret this, I had to think about what the spider means to me. So I *imagined* her weaving her web, and how she is held and supported by what she creates. I pictured her taking her time, and being patient as she worked on perfecting her creation. And I realised that I was getting the message to trust my own creative process writing this book, and that I too would be held and supported in this. To recap, here's how I was able to receive this message:

I took my time to *notice* the pattern or theme that was showing up in my life. I used my *imagination* to visualize the spider and feel more deeply into the message.
I *trusted* what my intuition showed me about what the spider was telling me.

Chapter Seven is on Decoding Your Messages and will give you a detailed step-by-step process on how to break down your intuitive messages.

NOTICING PATTERNS AND THEMES

Pay attention to the words you're using in conversations and the words other people are communicating to you. What words keep being repeated?

Look out for similar themes showing up in the TV shows and movies you're watching and the books you're reading.

Watch out for repetitive visuals or imagery in the world around you. Note them down so you remember.

Notice the music that feels like it's the soundtrack to your life. What are the lyrics of songs you find yourself singing along to?

What consistent feelings or emotions are showing up as a pattern or theme in your life? The more shadow based feelings like anger, anxiety or distrust can also be intuitive themes you're being asked to look at. Ask: what is the root of this? Why do I feel this way? Where in my life does it keep showing up? And remember to practice Energetic Self-Sovereignty, by asking: *are these feelings mine or someone else's?*

Never forget the power of slowing down, noticing and using your imagination to connect to your intuitive gifts—and now it's time to discover how your intuitive gifts like to work with you and how they're going to show up for you. The next chapter is going to help you to discover what your main gifts are and how you're naturally going to receive them. But first check out the following Intuitive Action points to guide you through stepping into a deeper practice of imagination and noticing.

‹‹‹‹‹‹

INTUITIVE ACTION

Here are some more ways to practice and become re-skilled in noticing and imagination. Slow down, take your time, and try these different exercises in the coming days.

Same Route Different Eyes

The next time you take a route that you use regularly—the journey to work, the drive to school, your favorite walk etc.—put yourself into the state of noticing and consciously take in all the details of the world around you. Allow yourself to be surprised by all the things you notice that you've never seen before.

Different Route New Eyes

Or switch it up completely! Instead of taking the same old route, consciously choose to go a different way. Take in all the new sights, sounds, and smells, as well as any feelings that come up when you take this detour from your usual routine. At the end of the journey note down or make a mental note of what you noticed and how your body felt taking this new route. If you received any intuitive guidance in this space of noticing note them down in your intuition journal.

Psychic Music Shuffle

Play a game to start noticing the intuitive messages in the music you listen to. Turn on your stereo and set it to shuffle. Now say out loud or in your head, "play me what I need to hear right now." Listen closely to whatever track it plays. What is the emotional quality of the music? What are the lyrics? What is the title of the song? Now, ask for a message and see what comes through. You can also do this by scrolling different stations on the radio, stopping at random, and noticing what's playing. This is one of my favorite things to do while I'm driving!

What's the Story?

Now let's activate your creative imagination! Pick one of the words below to begin, or come up with your own. Once you've picked a word, journal on what comes up for you around that word or create a short story. You can also simply close your eyes and allow yourself to visualize a story in your head. Whatever word you pick, flow with whatever comes up and try not to control how you think the story "should" go. Try and release all expectations. Follow what feels good in your body.

Dragon
Ocean

Star

Frog

Fast car

Tree

Cloud

Love

Skyscraper

Lightning bolt

Doctor

Creative Visualization

You can also use your imagination to tap into and express your feelings and emotions, and to "see" what messages they have for you. You'll need a pen and paper for this next exercise, and if you feel called you can go all out with colored pencils or paint. Take 10 minutes with this, or as long as you'd like. Pick a word or words from the list below, or choose one of your own. Now draw, write, doodle, or express whatever comes up for you when you feel into the energy of this word or words. Literally try to visualize or feel the word in your body. Notice any personal memories or emotions that come up for you when you begin to draw and imagine. When you've finished drawing, take in the image on the page. Ask yourself what you are being shown. How does this relate to what's happening in your life right now?

Fear

Anger

Busy mind

Calm

Trust

Connection

Happiness

Together

Myself

Others

You can also do this exercise by drawing how you feel right now in the present moment.

To do this, begin with the grounding visualization on page 52, and then simply start to draw.

GUIDED MEDITATION

The guided meditation for this chapter is for "Creative Imagination." It's designed to help you step into the space of noticing and reconnect you to your imagination, and you can find it in the online portal.

REPEAT TO INVOKE NOTICING AND IMAGINATION

I embrace the pause

I create the space

I release my guilt about slowing down

I open my whole energetic intuitive body to notice

I notice the magic all around me

I open myself up to experience the themes and patterns trying to get my attention

I reactivate my creative imagination

I unlock the power in my creative imagination

I step into the wonder of my creative imagination

I pause

I notice

I imagine

6

RECEIVING THE MESSAGES: WHAT ARE MY GIFTS?

Now that you're beginning to understand the language of your intuition, and how it speaks to you, the next piece of the puzzle is to begin to develop your own unique relationship to intuition. Because it's not a question of one gift fits all; we all receive our intuitive messages *differently* into our energetic intuitive body. Intuition is a full on sensory experience, involving our intuitive Seeing, Hearing, Feeling and Knowing gifts, as well as our taste and smell. One of these intuitive "senses" may be stronger in us, but we all have access to *ALL* these portals for receiving information. Practicing with them is how we unlock and create a deeper connection to our intuition.

You might have heard our intuitive gifts being called "the clairs" (after the French for "clear") especially in the New Age community. But I don't use this terminology, as it makes connecting to our intuition feel overly complicated, or as if you can only tap into this energy if you have "special powers." Which isn't the case, we all can access it at any time.

It's actually a common misconception that you will only receive a message one way, using one of the gifts. But our gifts tend to work together in unison. For example, you might receive your guidance using Feeling and Knowing at the same time; a heaviness in your body may alert you to something being off, and you also just "know" what's about to happen. In truth, separating out our Seeing, Hearing, Feeling and Knowing is just spiritual labeling, used to try and make this truly *numinous* process easier to understand. In fact, any time you get a message, it is being received by your whole energetic intuitive body, but you might only *experience* it as a feeling, or a knowing, or something you hear or see.

Some of the biggest blocks to receiving intuitive messages are frustration, comparison and perfection. But it's important not to compare yourself to others, or to expect your intuition to work in a certain way for you. Instead, the key is to learn to understand and work with your unique gifts. This means being open to how you receive information—which in turn means being patient with yourself as you remember and re-learn this ancient language. Sometimes we begin by getting to know one gift, allowing the others to come forward when they are ready. If you have perfectionist tendencies, you will also have to get comfortable with making mistakes and getting it "wrong." It takes time to reconnect to your intuition, and to discover how it likes to work with you, and so practice is key.

This chapter is a bit more practical, so take your time with it. In the coming pages I will break down each way you might receive your intuitive guidance, as well as show you how to create a deeper connection to each of your gifts. As you immerse yourself in this part of the work, notice which gift you feel naturally drawn to. This will help you to discover which gifts you are already working with, as well as the parts of your intuitive toolkit that you can work to develop over time.

INTUITIVE SEEING

Let's dive right in with Intuitive Seeing, which can be the gift that people are the most nervous about connecting to—simply because they are scared of what they "might" see. Books and movies have taught us to be fearful of seeing "ghosts" or encountering "dead people." Perhaps there is a fear of seeing something frightening that you then won't be able to *unsee*. Is this you? Are you worried about what you might see?

If any fear is present for you as we embark on this chapter, please go and re-read my author's note about ∞. The truth is, there are many different ways that Intuitive Seeing will show up to help you, that don't involve seeing spirits. In fact, you're probably already receiving messages through Intuitive Seeing without even realizing it.

For example, in the last chapter I showed you how to "*see*" guidance by noticing what's around you and seeing the signs and symbols in your everyday life. Intuitive Seeing can show up in our imagination too, helping us *"see"* imagery, words or symbols in our minds. You have also been using Intuitive Seeing in each of the guided visualizations I've led you through. Before we go further, let's discover if Intuitive Seeing is one of your stronger natural gifts.

Answer the questions below:

Do you consider yourself a visual person?
When you shut your eyes do you see pictures in your imagination?
Do you have vivid and colorful dreams?
Do you regularly notice signs, patterns, or symbols in your everyday environment?
Do you prefer to learn by being shown than being told?
Have you ever thought you might have seen a ghost or spirit?

If you answered YES to four or more of these questions you are naturally connected to your seeing gifts. If not, don't worry—you still have access to Intuitive Seeing, and I'm going to show you how to develop this.

HOW DO I "SEE" MY INTUITIVE MESSAGES?

As well as noticing signs, symbols, and patterns in the outside world, when you first connect to your seeing gifts, you might also see random flashes of color, notice a glowing light around people (their aura), or catch a movement out of the corner of your eye and wonder what it is. If this happens, trust that you are beginning to reactivate the gift of Intuitive Seeing.

The next step is to look beyond these external messages, and learn to "see" what your inner guidance system is showing you. Try this to begin to practice: as you read the words red apple, an image of a *red apple* will pop into your mind. You can see it. Now when you read *black dog wearing a yellow scarf* you will see an image of that dog in your head. You may need to close your eyes, but the image is there. Are you seeing the dog? This is how Intuitive Seeing brings us messages from within. We simply "see" an image in our head.

Some people receive messages from their Intuitive Seeing as a movie playing out in their mind. For others, it's as if a picture is appearing on a blank canvas or a screen. It can even show up as an image being projected out in front of a person. We're all different, and each of these ways of receiving guidance is "correct."

The below exercise will help you discover how *you* interact with Intuitive Seeing. First, re-familiarize yourself with the "energy faucet" exercise on page 50. As you progress through the exercise, go slow. Be patient. Notice. Trust what comes up for you. If you don't see anything at first, don't be disheartened. Simply try again.

THE EMPTY ROOM: SEEING

Get comfortable and close your eyes.

Do the Grounding Forcefield Visualization.

Imagine the "energy faucet" being turned on.

Now imagine yourself in an empty room. See it in your mind's eye. In this empty room you are going to be asked to SEE some intuitive messages.

If at any time you have trouble seeing something, imagine you have a torch in your hand which you can use to shine light into the empty room to make it clearer for you.

Now ask to be shown a color. Go with the first color that comes up for you. Trust what you're being shown. What color are you seeing? What does this color mean to you? Does it bring up any emotions?

Next, repeat out loud or in your head: *"I want to see a word or phrase. Let me see a word that might give me some guidance today."*

Imagine the word being written in the empty room. What is the word?

Trust what you are being shown. It might be a word or a phrase. Notice what it looks like. Is it being shown in a particular typeface? Are you seeing it like a movie? Or a cartoon? What does the word look like?

Now ask yourself, how does this word help me today? What is the message for me in this? (If you're not sure what it means, don't worry—we have a whole chapter coming up on how to help you decode your messages).

Now allow a symbol to appear in the empty room. What is the symbol? It could be a heart, a square, a star, a triangle. Trust what you're seeing. What does it mean to you? If you don't know what it means don't worry. Simply trust that you've seen it.

When you're ready, wiggle your hands and your toes and slowly open your eyes.

Note down anything you saw or experienced in your intuition journal. What messages did you receive?

If you didn't see anything in the empty room, go back and practice until you do. Take as long as you need. It can take multiple attempts. And if Intuitive Seeing still feels inaccessible to you, don't worry, we'll be trying this out for the other gifts, too.

INTUITIVE HEARING

So how do you *"hear"* intuitive messages? As we discussed in Chapter 4, your intuitive voice will sound just like your voice. It will come from the back of the head and will feel calm, centered and trustworthy—and this is the voice that will deliver guidance with Intuitive Hearing. Your job is to trust what it tells you.

When our Intuitive Hearing gets reactivated, you may become extra sensitive to the sounds around you. Background noises may seem much louder, as if the volume has been turned up on the sound of the dripping tap you've been meaning to get fixed, the electrical whirr of all the devices in your home, or your neighbor talking on the phone next door. You may even sometimes "hear" energy or get a buzzing in your ears with no explanation. Or hear someone call your name when there's nobody there. Developing your Intuitive Hearing is like tuning an old school radio—it's about learning how to distinguish the difference between your thoughts, all this background noise, and the intuitive voice that is sharing its messages with you.

Intuitive Hearing wasn't one of my strongest gifts. But over time, it is something that has come through stronger and stronger, to the point that now it's how I receive most of my own intuitive guidance as well as messages to share with others.

Before we look at how to develop it, let's see if Intuitive Hearing is one of your stronger natural gifts.

Answer the questions below:

Do you sometimes hear a song in your head and know it has a message for you?
Do you talk to yourself often?
Do you find yourself using the phrase "I hear" in conversations? For example: "I hear what you're saying."
Do you sometimes hear a light buzzing or feel energy around your ears?
Can you hear a voice in your head that sounds like it is guiding you?
Have you ever heard your name being spoken when nobody else is around?

If you answered YES to four or more of the questions you are naturally connected to your Intuitive Hearing. If not, don't worry, you still have access to this gift.

By the way, did you answer "yes" to the question about talking to yourself? If so, maybe you felt slightly ashamed of this, as we've been taught that it's "weird" to do this. But it's actually very normal to talk to ourselves, and if you're somebody who does this regularly, you're actually more open to receiving guidance through Intuitive Hearing. It means you're already used to vocalizing and hearing your inner intuitive voice.

WHY ARE MY EARS BUZZING?

When my hearing gifts got reactivated I wondered if I had the medical condition tinnitus, as I was hearing so much buzzing. Now, when my ears start to buzz, I know that my intuition is trying to get my attention. ∞ is letting me know that I'm not listening to something, or that a loved one who has passed is letting me know they're around. When this happens to you, acknowledge the buzzing you're experiencing and say out loud or in your head, "What are you trying to say? I'm here to listen." Pause and make space to receive the intuitive message that wants to come through. Once this happens the buzzing will most likely stop. If it continues it can also be that you are experiencing buzzing as a reactivation symptom.

So let's connect you to your Intuitive Hearing and help you strengthen this connection. We're going to use the same Empty Room exercise but this time for our hearing.

THE EMPTY ROOM: HEARING

Get comfortable and close your eyes.

Do the Grounding Forcefield Vizualization.

Imagine the "energy faucet" being turned on.

Imagine yourself in an empty room. In this empty room we are going to be asked to HEAR some intuitive messages.

Take a moment to listen to the noises all around you right now. What can you hear?

You will be able to hear more than one sound at once. What different things can you hear?

Try focusing on one sound at a time. What can you hear in your space? What can you hear outside?

Now we're going to bring in our sound memories into the empty room.

Imagine the sound of a ticking clock.
Imagine the wind blowing through trees
Imagine a time in your life that brought you happiness and joy. Imagine yourself back there. What noises were around you?

Now imagine you're in a crowd in a large stadium full of people. Hear all the noises around you.
Your friend is standing next to you. They are talking to you but it's hard to hear over the noise of the crowd. Imagine yourself tuning into what they are saying to you. Focus on their voice and imagine the background noise fading out. What is your friend saying? Can you just hear their voice?

Now let's try and get some intuitive guidance by hearing.

Say out loud, or in your head: *"I want to hear a word or phrase. Let me hear a word that might give me some guidance today."*

What do you hear? If you can't hear anything, ask to hear it louder and clearer. Trust what comes through and go with the first thing you heard. It might just be one word or a whole phrase. Now ask yourself, how does this help me today? What is the message for me?

When you're ready, wiggle your hands and your toes and slowly open your eyes.

Note down anything you heard or experienced in your intuition journal. What messages did you receive?

If you didn't hear anything in the empty room, go back and repeat and practice until you do. Take as long as you need. It can take multiple attempts. In your day-to-day life, you can practice strengthening your Intuitive Hearing by simply tuning in to the different sounds and noises around you. When you're listening to music, try to hear all the different instruments. If you're out in your town or city, consciously choose to "hear" each car, siren, or person talking in the street. Or have some listening time for a few minutes laying in bed when you wake up or go to sleep. These are all great ways to strengthen your connection to your hearing gifts.

INTUITIVE KNOWING

It's easy to overlook simply *knowing* as a way we might receive intuitive guidance. Unlike the other gifts, *knowing* isn't one of the traditional senses we use to interact with the outside world, it's an inner sense. For this reason, it might be something you see as simply part of who you are, versus part of your intuition. And your Intuitive Knowing is an important way to connect to your intuitive truth and power. It shows up when you just "know" you should apply for a certain job, or that there's a problem with a contract, or that you should stay away from a certain individual. However, Intuitive Knowing is trickier to develop as it requires a deeper level of trust in yourself and what you believe to be true.

Before we learn how to develop your Intuitive Knowing, let's discover if this is one of your stronger natural gifts.

Answer the questions below:

Do you know things about people before you learn about them?
Do you find yourself saying "I know" in conversations?
Do you find you just know when to stay away from someone?
Do friends and family comment to you and wonder how you just "know" things?
Are you naturally drawn to trust your inner knowing?
Do you ever feel like you know something is going to happen, and then it does?

If you answered YES to four or more of the questions you are naturally connected to your Intuitive Knowing. If not, don't worry, you still have access to this gift. Let's use the Empty Room exercise again to strengthen this connection.

THE EMPTY ROOM: KNOWING

Close your eyes.

Do the Grounding Forcefield Visualization

Imagine the "energy faucet" being turned on.

Imagine yourself in an empty room. See it in your mind's eye. In this empty room you are going to be asked to KNOW some intuitive messages.

Put your hands on your solar plexus energy center—located an inch above your belly button.

Take a few deep breaths and breath into this energy center filling it with your breath.

Imagine a golden light entering the empty room and imagine it entering into your body where your hands are. Imagine this golden light filling up your solar plexus energy center, filling up this place of knowing, trust, and self-worth. How does it feel in your body?

Now remember a time in your life when you just "knew" something to be true. An inner knowing about a person or a situation. Visualize it in the empty room.

Next, feel into where this knowing came from in your body. Was it your heart? Your solar plexus? Your head? Or somewhere else?

Using your memory, picture what happened when you took action on that knowing guidance. What was the impact or outcome of you trusting and acting on your Intuitive Knowing? Reflect on this event.

When you're ready, take a few deep breaths. Wiggle your hands and your toes and slowly open your eyes.

Note down in your intuition journal how it felt to have the golden energy enter your solar plexus, and where you felt your Intuitive Knowing in your body. Make a note of anything else that came up about trusting and taking action on your knowing gifts.

This time, the Empty Room exercise was about helping you recall what your Intuitive Knowing feels like in your body, and what happens when you trust your knowing. You can take this a step further by keeping a section in your intuition journal where you write down all the "knowing" messages you have received in your life, the actions you took, and how things turned out when your followed your intuition.

As you look back and reflect on the outcomes, positive or negative, this will likely bring to light some interesting patterns and themes around how you work with your Intuitive Knowing.

INTUITIVE FEELING

In Chapter Three we spoke about the power of Energetic Self-Sovereignty and touched on how identifying as an empath is actually part of our Intuitive Feeling. There can be a lot of shame in identifying as an empath or a highly sensitive person. You may have been told that, "You're too sensitive!"—leading you to see this quality as negative or somehow a burden on others. But this is where we get to reframe having big feelings as an intuitive superpower! Because the very same feelings are another way we connect to our energetic intuitive body, and discover what it's trying to share with us on a daily basis.

Before we go into discovering how to develop your Intuitive Feeling, let's see if *"feeling"* is one of your stronger natural gifts.
Answer the following questions:

When you walk into a room of people does it feel overwhelming as if you can feel everyone else's emotions?
Do you consider yourself a sensitive person?

Do you avoid conflict with others when it could get emotional?
Do you need lots of alone time to recharge?
Do you have trouble distinguishing between your emotions and those that belong to someone else?
Do you get emotional at big events such as weddings and parties?
Do you pick up on the "vibe" of different buildings or spaces?

If you answered YES to four or more of the questions you are naturally connected to your Intuitive Feeling. If not, don't worry—you still have access to these feeling gifts.

The question when it comes to Intuitive Feeling, is how to tell the difference between feelings as guidance versus an emotional reaction to something in the outside world. One way is to use Intuitive Feeling to receive a "Hell Yes" or a "Heck No" answer to a question. We will all receive this differently, but with a "Hell Yes" you may feel warmth, tingles, or a light breeze. You might feel it in a certain part of your body. It might feel really good and like your whole body is being lit up with this "Hell Yes" energy. You might also get some Intuitive Seeing messages too—for example, the color green for "go," or a set of traffic lights with the green light lit up.

If it's a "Heck No" the sensations will be different. You might feel the energy shut off, or your body go cold. You may feel it in a different part of your body. Again you might also get some Intuitive Seeing messages at the same time, and see the color red for "stop," or even see a stop sign.

Once you discover what these feeling guides are for you, you can use them to help you in all sorts of different situations. It might be something as simple as, "Do I take this job? Or buy that new pair of shoes?" It may be something more general, such as "Should I take action or wait?" Eventually, you may be able to receive guidance from Intuitive Feeling when ∞ is trying to show you whether something bigger and less easy to define is a "yes" or a "no" in your life. You can also use Intuitive Feeling to help you decode messages (as we will discover in the next chapter) and share messages with others.

For now, let's try the empty room exercise to connect you to your Intuitive Feeling, and discover what a "Hell Yes" or "Heck No" feeling is for you in your energetic intuitive body. Remember, we all experience this differently!

THE EMPTY ROOM: FEELING

Close your eyes.

Do the Grounding Forcefield Visualization.

Imagine the "energy faucet" being turned on.

Imagine yourself in an empty room. See it in your mind's eye. In this empty room we are going to be asked to FEEL some intuitive messages.

Take a few deep breaths into your whole energetic body. Use this breath to tune into your body and see how your body feels in the present moment.

Notice how your body physically feels. Relaxed? Calm? Tense? Are you holding any tension anywhere in the body? Breathe into those parts to release the tension.

Notice how your body feels when you breathe into these parts. Does it feel lighter? Does it feel balanced?

Now notice how you feel emotionally right now. How do you feel today? Allow the feelings to arise. Notice them. Be honest with yourself about how you feel. Notice the physical feelings and sensations that come up for you in your body. No need to label them, just notice they are there.

Next, imagine a white light enter the room and move into your intuitive body. Breathe it into your whole body. How does it feel?

Now we're going to tune into your intuitive body so you can use Intuitive Feeling to find your Hell Yes or Heck No guidance.

Ask to be shown a "Hell Yes" in your body.

What does it feel like? What sensations are coming up?
Tune into the small subtleties in your intuitive body.
Do you feel warmth, tingles or a light breeze?
Can you feel it in a certain part of your body or your whole body?
What does this "Hell Yes" energy feel like for you?

Now ask to be shown a "Heck No" in your body.

What does it feel like? What sensations are coming up?
Again tune into the small subtleties in your intuitive body.
Do you feel the energy get shut off, your body feel cold, or a feeling in your heart?
Can you feel it in a certain part of your body or your whole body?
What does this "Heck No" energy feel like for you?

Once you have your "Heck No," connect to the "Hell Yes" energy again in the empty room. Ask it to step forward again so you can feel the difference between the two.

When you're ready, take a few deep breaths. Wiggle your hands and your toes and slowly open your eyes.

Note down the details of what you felt for your Hell Yes or Heck No guidance in your intuition journal. This is so you can remember what it feels like, for next time you want to use this tool. You can use this technique to help you with decisions on a daily basis. You may be amazed how much you go to say yes to that is actually a Heck No for you!

◇◇◇◇◇

Did you like the "empty room" exercise? You can begin each day with this, to begin to practice calling on your different intuitive gifts. If you have a question that needs answering, you can also step into the empty room any time to ask for guidance. As always, practice trusting and acting on what comes up for you. You can also access the Empty Room exercises in the online portal.

But also remember that you might receive guidance from a combination of two or more of the gifts all at once. As mentioned earlier, separating out the gifts is spiritual labeling, and simply makes them easier to understand. Your whole energetic body is also receiving the guidance, so you might not even be able to identify clearly "where" it is coming from. Be open to the fact that you might get a feeling, see something, and know something all at once.

If you struggled with one of the exercises or gifts, don't give up. Try the exercises again and most importantly remember to have fun with it! ∞ is always reminding us that this doesn't need to be "serious work" and that when it becomes too serious we need to step back into the energy of play, joy and childlike wonder.

On your journey to reactivate your gifts, you might also discover that you receive guidance in your dreams (which are another portal to Intuitive Seeing and Intuitive Feeling). You may discover you have intuitive smelling or tasting gifts too. How we receive our intuitive guidance is always adapting and evolving, and there's also no "end point" to aim for. In fact, there will always be more to learn as you connect more deeply to your inner truths.

For now, the next step is discovering how to understand and decode what the intuitive messages being streamed in your direction mean. This is when you learn how to use this incredible guidance and take back your power in your everyday life.

◇◇◇◇◇

GUIDED MEDITATION

The guided meditation for this chapter is a repeat of the Empty Room exercises so you can repeat them to practice and gain confidence in connecting to your gifts. You can find it in the online portal.

REPEAT TO INVOKE RECEIVING INTUITIVE GUIDANCE

I receive the full spectrum of my gifts

I am unique and my guidance comes my way

I will not force how ∞ wants to work with me

I release perfection and the desire to get it right

I receive in the empty room and step into the magic

I surrender and trust what is shown to me

I am hearing

I am seeing

I am knowing

I am feeling

∞

7

DECODE YOUR MESSAGES: BE THE DETECTIVE

Okay, so here's where things get personal ... and maybe a little bit daunting! You're getting a message ... but how are you supposed to *act* on your intuition if you're unsure what the guidance is trying to tell you? It's like meeting the love of your life and then realizing you don't speak the same language. You spend half the time trying to work out what the other person is trying to say and the other half questioning your own interpretation of it. Another block to us living from our intuition is the fear that we're going to mess it up and get the meaning of a message wrong.

It's also super frustrating to receive a message, something you know is important and you know is meant just for YOU, but you have no idea what it means. Your heart sinks, and your mind goes into overdrive as doubt and fear kick in: *"Maybe it's not my intuition after all?"* Faced with uncertainty about the next right move to take, a tendency to overthink can even drive us to withdraw further from life, and to fall back into comfortable but limiting old patterns. In our confusion, we tell ourselves that working with our intuition is "too complicated." But it really isn't.

This chapter is going to help you to *"Be the Detective"* and learn to decode and trust your own intuitive guidance. It will show you how to bring out your inner sleuth and take action in your life.

WHAT DOES IT MEAN TO ME?

Decoding a message is this simple:

Receive the intuitive hit.

Pause.

Reflect.

And ask yourself: *What does it mean to me?*

That's literally it, your job then being to simply follow where your thoughts and feelings take you.

How does it work? We all have our own "Inner Reference Library," a bank of images, sounds, and other sensory impressions that have been logged in our memory as we've experienced life. Everything you've ever encountered in this lifetime, from childhood right up to the present day, has also been infused with "meaning" by your psyche, which means each of the colors, smells, tastes, visuals, and emotions in the world mean something specific to you. All of which is collated in your Inner Reference Library. Decoding your intuitive guidance is simply about accessing this library, to discover the "hidden" personal meaning in whatever message you are seeing, hearing, or feeling. This means there is nothing "new" for you to learn; rather, it is about drawing deeply from your own well of wisdom and experience. Once put into action, you'll surprise yourself how much life changing insight you have actually had access to all along.

If you want, you can add another layer of depth to the process by considering that you've also had multiple past life experiences. Every experience from every life you've lived leaves its unique imprint in your Inner Reference Library too, and when your soul incarnates in a new body you take this information with you. Rather than this being overwhelming, simply consider the incredible breadth of understanding and knowledge that you have access to.

Back to how this works when you receive a message, and have asked yourself: *What does this mean to me?* You don't need any special skills to access your Inner Reference Library, it will happen naturally. The key is to simply pause, take a moment to reflect, and to trust whatever symbols, words, signs and feelings come up from your memory bank. When you ask: *What does this mean to me?* you are inviting the message to enter your energetic intuitive body. As you get more practiced at this, you'll be able to decode your messages quicker and with greater accuracy.

The next step is to consider what area of your life the message relates to. You might know instantly. It's the family argument you're in the middle of, or the tricky dynamic with your boss you're experiencing. But if it isn't obvious, the next question to ask yourself is: *"What part of my life is this guidance for?"* Then, as above, take a moment to pause and trust whatever comes up. By asking this question, you are creating another strand of connection between the message and your Inner Reference Library. Working with a message like this is like peeling back the layers of an onion, or opening all of the Russian dolls stacked inside one another. Eventually you will reach the center and the truth of the message.

Once you have these two pieces of information—what the message means to you, and the area of your life it applies to—you can begin to take action on your guidance. If you're still unsure, there's no need to rush into anything. Simply continue to reflect on what has come up and allow the message to sink in. It's also very normal for parts of the message not to make any sense at all—like when you have a dream that has a powerful meaning, but is also peppered with lots of small details that seem irrelevant.

As we've already learned, everyone receives their intuitive guidance in their own unique way, and this applies to how we decode our messages too. Your intuition is your very own, one of a kind, extrasensory superpower. So take your time and be patient with yourself as you practice to decode your messages. It's like you've been driving a regular car for years ... and then being given a car that flies! It looks identical on the outside, but very quickly you discover it has a whole new set of levers and buttons, including ones that can take you into the stratosphere! Remember, you don't have to be an expert at this right off the bat. Take your time, stay curious, and be kind with yourself.

YOU ARE YOUR OWN SEARCH ENGINE

Technology is upgrading and changing how we live our lives, with the Internet having revolutionized how we access information. Connected as a global community by our smartphones, the entire history of the world and the thoughts of 7.5 billion people (and counting) are all at our finger-tips. But this in turn is impacting our ability to decode the meaning of our personal intuitive messages. We're so used to tapping our questions into Google, the oracle of the modern world, we're not used to working with our Inner Reference Library.

Not only do we want answers on demand, we've also learned to out-source responsibility for our actions and the choices we make based on external information. Our busy lives are so overscheduled, it may feel like you don't have time to pause and reflect to decipher a message from ∞. In some cases, we've just become plain lazy. Why do the work of figuring something out for myself when I can just ask someone else?

And this applies as much to answers about our emotional and spiritual lives, as to practical information about how to dress and what to eat. The Internet also gives us access to thousands of articles, posts and videos on every spiritual or self-help topic under the sun. You want to learn how to lucid dream? Check out this YouTube clip. Need to know if energy healing can help you? Read this blog post. Which is amazing, as it's made ∞ more accessible to millions of people. But if you're using the Internet to help you decode personal intuitive messages, you are most likely decoding your messages wrong.

Check out this example. You wake one morning after a vivid dream in which you were out with friends when suddenly you noticed your teeth had started to fall out. You felt confused and embarrassed. Looking down, you saw six teeth in the palm of your hand. As the details begin to slip away from you, you roll over with one eye open and head online for the answer. "Dream meaning teeth falling out?" You'll probably find online a short two sentence answer telling you that teeth falling out relates to a sense of loss, or means you're worried or anxious about something. But if this doesn't resonate, you might actually be left feeling even more puzzled and disoriented. It might open up bigger questions: *Why were these friends in the dream too? Why were there specifically six teeth? Why was I embarrassed in the dream?*

We're decoding our messages wrong online because these meanings usually refer to universal symbols of the global collective. Passed on from generation to generation, ancestor to ancestor, these have their roots in myths about how humans have lived on this planet over the millenia. A way to find common ground and communicate with each other, these universal meanings aren't a bad thing as they come from the collective reference library that we all tap into. But the fact it's so easy to look these meanings up online now, means our ability to work with our own individual meanings is slowly being eroded and forgotten.

Let's look at the universal symbol of a star to highlight this point. A star can represent dreams, fame, a journey, success, or uniqueness. But the way the star is drawn can also change its meaning. A five-pointed star, known as a Pentagram, is associated with the pagan practices and traditions of Wicca. Its five points represent the four elements (water, fire, air, and earth) with the fifth and top point representing "spirit." The six-pointed star, a hexagram, is the religious symbol for Judaism. It's known as the Star of David and has its own religious meanings. See how one seemingly simple symbol can have so many different meanings?

It's the same for colors. If you go online and search: *"What does the color yellow mean?"* you will be served hundreds of options. On one hand, yellow depicts sunshine, hope, and happiness. But it can also mean cowardice, deceit and sickness. Not to mention that colors also have cultural meanings depending on where you are in the world. In Egypt, yellow is the color of mourning, and in Japan it means courage.

So beware of heading straight online to get your answers. Yes, they can provide insight and be helpful to a degree. But our individual messages from ∞ are personal whispers to us, and only us. They are not meant for the collective. They are intimate and exclusive and they contain details and nuances that only we can decode. They are designed to empower us to access our *own* inner truth and power. When we learn how to trust our own interpretations, we literally learn how to know our own minds—and make choices and take actions that are in alignment with who we truly are.

USING TOOLS TO HELP YOU BE THE DETECTIVE

All you truly need to decode your intuitive guidance is YOU and the signs around you. But spiritual tools like oracle or tarot card decks can support you in receiving your guidance. However, it's important not to rely on these tools. If you're someone that regularly uses oracle decks, when was the last time you decoded the meaning of the card using your own Inner Reference Library? Or do you alway head to the little book to find the meaning?

There's no shame in this—most of us rely on the book that comes with a deck with all the descriptions of what each card means. But essentially this means we are giving our power to whatever the author wrote about the *universal* meaning. *Next time you find yourself pulling cards, searching again for answers outside yourself, try this exercise instead:*

Before looking at the image on the card, hold it in your hand face down and ask yourself, *"how does this card make me feel?"* Use your Feeling and Seeing gifts, notice what images, sensations or feelings you are receiving from the card. Get your intuitive guidance without even looking at it. Be the detective. When you're ready turn the card over and see what other insight you can get from the picture or what's written in the book.

If the description of the card doesn't tally with the intuitive guidance you've already received, choose to trust your own guidance. You will always get more messages when you work with your card decks this way.

It's also important to notice when you become reliant on your cards instead of listening to your intuitive voice. Do you feel like you always turn to your cards to keep you on track and make decisions? If so, step away. Sometimes we need to be in the uncomfortable space of not knowing so that the next time we do receive intuitive guidance on something we can tell right away that it's a Hell Yes!

THE DECODING IS IN THE DETAILS

The key to decoding a message in a way that is completely unique to you is to pay attention to the details. This is because each of these details will have its own specific meaning stored away in your personal Inner Reference Library. Let's use the example of the dog with the yellow scarf from the last chapter to look at how this works.

Begin with the dog:

Picture the dog, seeing it in your imagination or the empty room

What kind of dog is it? Do you know what breed it is?
Is it a large dog with teeth that you find scary?
Or a small dog that's all fluffy and playful?
Is the dog well groomed or is it unkempt and covered in mud?
How does the dog make you feel from what you're being shown?

And now let's consider the scarf:

What shade of yellow is it? Is it more golden yellow or is it luminous?
Is it tied in a bow, or loosely slung over the dog's back?
Is there a pattern on it?
Is it made from expensive looking material or something cheaper?
How does the scarf make you feel?

Can you see how your answers to these questions—which will always be unique to you—are already giving you so much more information about what your message means? Depending on the mood the dog is in, or the way the scarf is tied, it can go from being an image reminding you to be more playful and carefree, to a message asking you to look at what you're scared of in your life right now, or where you could benefit from getting more organized.

Now let's take it one step further.

FOLLOW THE TRAIL

Once you've noticed the details, and accessed your Inner Reference Library to decode what they mean to you, the next step is to follow the trail. This is how we begin to interact with the guidance we're receiving, to get more information about how it applies to our situation. The way to do this is to ask questions. Have a read of the example below on how to do this.

Amy, a successful writer in her thirties, was enjoying the summer sunshine in her garden. Over the space of a few days she saw two dead birds in her garden. She was sad for the birds but knew they were a sign. Instead of searching online she followed the trail of the message. First she looked up "birds" in her Inner Reference Library. She realized that birds represented freedom to her, one of the most important values in her life. She then looked up "death"—and realized that, to her, this symbolized new beginnings.

This led her to examine where in her life she was craving freedom and new beginnings. Now she had more clarity on what the message meant: she had recently moved to a new city, but after a few months had realized she actually wanted to settle somewhere else. She felt trapped, stuck in a rut, and still craved the freedom she had hoped to find in her move. The dead birds were a message that it was okay to change her living situation again.

Amy continued following the trail, as the fact she had seen two birds told her there was a second meaning to the message. She asked, " what does the second bird mean to me?" She was single but immediately felt the second bird represented an ex who she was still in contact with. She knew he also felt trapped in his current life situation. She asked her intuition if she should help him. When she listened to how this felt in her body, she got the answer "No." The second dead bird was a reminder that the relationship was dead and that her ex must create his own freedom.

Working with her intuition this way, Amy felt empowered to make the necessary changes in her living situation and started looking for new places straight away. She also knew that she had to stop being in contact with her ex.

Let's look at what this story shows us about combining the techniques and tools we've been discussing in the last few chapters to receive and decode your own intuitive guidance.

The power of *noticing* allowed Amy to see the two birds as an intuitive message for her. She then stepped into the space of imagination and asked herself: *"What does it mean to me?"* She didn't go online but paused, reflected, and accessed her *Inner Reference Library* to find the meaning of the message. She then *followed* the trail, by asking: *"What's going on in my life that this is guidance for?"* Once she had discovered the meaning and area of her life she used the "Hell Yes / Heck No" technique to ask her intuition a question so she could gain even more clarity on her situation. The icing on the cake was that Amy then took action on the guidance she received. She didn't ignore it or doubt it. She trusted her intuition and began to make the changes she knew would help her take back her power and be in her truth.

THE INTUITIVE "INSTANT HIT"

Sometimes when we receive an intuitive hit we instantly know exactly what it means and what action to take. But other times it can take days, weeks or even years to decode a message. It can be frustrating when we don't have the full answer straight away, as it challenges the way we have been conditioned to want and expect instant gratification. But don't let this put you off. Trust that time takes its own time and that you'll get your answer when you're ready.

Time for a bit of a truth bomb: *You're not going to be able to decode every message you get*. This is because sometimes part of the intuitive process is the not knowing. Or sometimes you will get your answer, just not how you expect. More often than not this happens when you surrender and allow a message to breathe. You'll go about your life and suddenly out of nowhere the lightbulb moment, like finding the answer to a crossword clue that's been bugging you for days: "Ohhhhhh that's what it means!!?? I get it now." Trust time. Trust your intuition. Trust yourself.

Even better, in the next chapter you're going to discover how to get some cosmic help along the way—as I introduce you to the Spirit Team and Ancestors who are supporting you on this path.

◇◇◇◇◇

INTUITIVE ACTION

Use these simple exercises to get familiar with your Inner Reference Library, as you become the detective and decode your intuitive guidance.

Symbols

Practice decoding these common symbols by simply asking yourself: *"What does it mean to me?"* Trust the first thing that comes up, versus what you "know" about each symbol. Make a note in your Intuition Journal.

Heart
Pyramid
Eye
Star
Fire
Arrow
Cross
Crescent moon
Circle
Labrinth
Skull

Animals

Now try the same with these animals, again asking yourself: *"What does it mean to me?"* It may mean more than one thing, for example: *"A dove represents countryside, childhood, someone about to pass over."*

Dove
Spider
Lion
Bear
Whale
Butterfly
Eagle
Dog

Owl

Elephant

Colors

Colors are so powerful and different shades of one color can have various meanings. For example, one shade of red can mean danger but another can mean passion! Only you will know what each shade represents for you.

When you see different shades of a color consciously ask yourself what they mean to you. You can do this by looking at the different shades of the fruits and vegetables at the supermarket, or the different colors of the books at a book store, or the shades of paint for sale at a home improvement shop.

The next time you receive these different colors through Intuitive Seeing you'll know what their message is for you.

Feelings

This exercise will help you remember how certain emotions "feel" in the body. Next time a message comes with a strong emotion, or physical sensation, you will have a reference for it.

Get comfortable and close your eyes.

Go back into The Empty Room from the last chapter.

Imagine a time in your life when you felt happy. Go with the first memory. Take in this moment. What is happening? Where do you feel happiness in your body? What is the physical sensation?

Imagine a time in your life when you felt angry. Go with the first memory. Take in this moment. What is happening? Where do you feel anger in your body? What is the physical sensation?

Imagine a time in your life when you felt alone. Go with the first memory.

Take in this moment. What is happening? Where do you feel loneliness in your body? What is the physical sensation?

Imagine a time in your life when you felt love or received love. Go with the first memory. Take in this moment. What is happening? Where do you feel love in your body? What is the physical sensation?

When you're ready, take a few deep breaths. Wiggle your hands and your toes and slowly open your eyes.

Note down in your intuition journal what you felt for each emotion, where it showed up in your body, and the physical sensation of it. You can repeat this for as many different emotions as you like.

Follow The Trail

Do you have a particular area that you'd like some guidance on right now? Think of a question you'd like to ask, relating to career, relationships, finance, love, or health. Now let's go back into the Empty Room.

Get comfortable and close your eyes.

Imagine yourself in the Empty Room. Ask your question out loud or in your head. Ask to receive some guidance on this question.

Once you've received a message through your Intuitive Seeing, Hearing, Feeling, or Knowing, go to your Inner Refence Library to decode what it means. The first step is to ask, *"What does it mean to me?"*

Once you get an answer, follow the trail for more insight (like Amy did in the story above). Keep asking questions until you feel you've got the full answer.

Once you feel complete, write the question and answer down in your intuition journal and consider what actions you could take to follow this guidance in your life.

GUIDED MEDITATION

The guided meditation for this chapter is to help you "Access Your Inner Reference Library." It's designed to help you connect to your answer book and discover what any symbols and signs mean for you. You can find it in the online portal.

REPEAT TO INVOKE YOUR INTUITIVE DETECTIVE

I can crack the code of my intuition

I am the detective of my guidance

I ask what it means to me

I open my inner reference library

I notice the details

I follow the trail

I trust what the guidance means for me

I take action to step into my intuitive power

I am the detective and I uncover my truth

∞

8

CALL ON YOUR SPIRIT TEAM

The next step in your intuitive journey is to meet your "Spirit Team." That's right. There's a whole team "out there" to help guide and shield you, so you can be in your Energetic Self-Sovereignty. This Spirit Team is made up of your spirit guides, your ancestors, and any loved ones who have gone to the other side, and that have intuitive wisdom to share with you too.

This team is here to support us as we navigate our human journey. With practice, we develop a special intimate bond with them, so that when we come to recognize their presence it is magical, calming, and acts as encouragement for us to step into our power. Working with our Spirit Team lets us know we're never alone, and that we're supported every step of the way. The same way a solo singer has their back up vocalists and band for support, or an athlete can feel the energetic support of the home crowd willing them on.

We've all reincarnated and lived multiple different lives before this one, and our Spirit Team can also be made up of the people we've encountered on this epic path through the Cosmos. So when we experience their presence in this lifetime, it can also trigger a deep remembrance of our past lives. This alone connects us more deeply to our intuitive power, to our truth, and to our unique relationship to ∞.

Your Spirit Team is always changing and evolving, and new members of this team will step forward to support you through different phases and chapters of your life. If this is all new to you, and you're wondering how you've made it this far in life without hearing from them, your team has been hanging out in the background until you've ready to consciously work with them. This chapter is dedicated to how you can discover who they are, call them forward, and learn how they can help you.

But let's be clear. They're here to teach you, not to lead you. They're here to guide you, not to wrap you up in cotton wool and protect you from the tough lessons that are part of this human experience. Remember, it's part of our societal conditioning to look for external guidance versus connect to our own inner power, and to look to the outside for validation. So beware of relying heavily on this Spirit Team. Let their wisdom and support be an add-on to you accessing your own gifts and inner truths.

But wait, isn't this a contradictory message? I've been telling you throughout this book that YOU are your own best resource, and other self-help teachers are always telling you to trust yourself before turning to others for validation. Plus it can also feel super awkward asking for help. We've been conditioned to be hyper independent, and many of us feel vulnerable asking for help from our friends, family and community. But in a way, your Spirit Team is an extension of you, embodying ephemeral parts of your past, present, and future selves. And the same way we feel more secure having people in our lives we know we can rely on without even really having to ask, learning to work in harmony with their energy can help us feel energetically supported, ever safer to be ourselves, and more deeply in tune with our own intuition.

It can feel a bit overwhelming when you come to understand there is this team around you. It can bring up feelings of not trusting the unknown and doubts as to whether or not something is real. It can also bring up questions like, *"Are they always watching me then? If I'm having sex or on the toilet does this mean I'm never alone?"* (Answer: NO! They're not always spying on you.) So if you're feeling a little challenged or uncertain by this concept, please keep reading.

YOUR SPIRIT GUIDES

The Guides on our Spirit Team are here to help us evolve and to hold our hand on our life journey. That is, the journey to discover who we truly

CALL ON YOUR SPIRIT TEAM

are and why we're here. Your Guides can appear as humans, non human beings, animals, or even just in energetic form. It can be said that once you've learned everything you are here to learn in human form, your soul can become a Spirit Guide and help others in this role.

While we can have many guides in our Spirit Team, we all have one principal Guide—a little like the "daemons" from the *His Dark Materials* books and TV series by Phillip Pullman. With us from birth until the time that we die, just like us they have their own gifts, talents, passions, and personality, and they use these talents to help us and to connect with us. Chances are your Guide has been with you in multiple lifetimes. They know you on a deep soul level, and if your tie has been severed, for whatever reason, reconnecting with them is a very special experience. It's hard to put into "human" words, but imagine reconnecting to a never ending love that exists outside of you, and that transcends all time and space. I'll be showing you how in a minute.

Your main Guide may also be the representation of somebody who is part of your ancestral lineage. However, loved ones you knew in this life before they passed over can't be your main Guide—due to the fact they were alive at the time you were born. But deceased loved ones *are* looking out for you from the afterlife. So if you've had a really special relationship with a relative or a friend who's passed, they can be part of your Spirit Team.

Besides our main Guide and our Ancestors (who we'll learn more about below) we can also get support from entities from different planets. Known as "Starseeds," these are advanced beings from a different star or galaxy. This might sound pretty far out, but there's nothing to be afraid of. The mainstream media and movie industry has conditioned us to see beings from different planets as only part of our imagination, threatening, or not believable. We're fed stories that extraterrestrials are here to take over the world and to fear alien abductions, when actually the benevolent Starseeds are trying to help us. These beings join our Spirit Team to help us evolve, to grow as humans, and to play our role in the evolution of the collective.

Remember how I told you I had my first encounter with what I've come to know as my main Spirit Guide aged five? She appeared at the end of my bed one night when I was feeling scared and said to me: "Don't be afraid. I'm here to guide you and protect you." She appeared as a glowing light with icy blue energy emanating from her, but the most vivid memory I have of this experience is simply that I felt safe and looked after. I labelled her as "female" because her energy felt feminine to me. Over the years I've cultivated a relationship with her, where I know what her energy feels like, how she shows herself to me, and even the tone of her voice (when she's trying to get my attention and I'm not listening it can be a little blunt).

But from the moment we "met," I felt she knew me and saw me on a deeper level than anybody had before. The first night she came to me, I felt like she saw my essence and understood my soul. I knew her love was limitless and unconditional and the energy in my heart space felt full. Not that I had the language for this aged 5, but I can still feel it when I think back to that moment. It wasn't until I began attending the psychic circles at age 16 that I reconnected with her. She appeared to me again in a guided meditation as I reactivated my intuitive gifts, and I felt the same level of love and connection. It was as if she was saying, "Remember me? Remember how it feels to connect to your power?" As I said, when you connect to your main Guide it can be an emotionally powerful experience. Like remembering a forgotten love, or getting a glimpse of a past life, and accompanied by a deep sense of knowing and familiarity.

The same way my main Guide came into my life when she knew I was ready, different members of our team will show up to work with us at certain times in our lives to give us guidance around specific problems or life goals. You may also meet new members of your Spirit Team when you visit different parts of the world. Sometimes you can carry their energy with you when you head home, but their guidance and protection can also be specific to that place. As you shapeshift and evolve through your life, your team will shift and evolve with you. Except for your main Guide, who will always be there when you need them.

When we discover our main Guide, we can also get some insight into why we might have been drawn to or felt a connection to a particular place in the world or a time in history, or why we love a certain color, movie, or art piece. For example you might have a fascination with the ancient Egyptians and discover your main Guide is from there. Or you've always wanted to travel to Italy and you discover your Guide has lived there. Or your favorite color has always been purple, and when your Guide shows up they have a purple energy. This information has all been stored away in your personal Inner Reference Library, waiting for you to reach the point in your life when you are ready to receive it.

I connected with a new Guide when I first moved to the land that is now known as Vancouver, Canada. Feeling lost and ungrounded as I adapted to my new home, I needed support to feel I'd made the right decision to move. I was in the middle of a meditation connecting to ∞, looking for guidance, when a First Nation guide, whose land I was now on, stepped forward to help me transition. He first reminded me that this was his land, and that I was not to forget the cultural legacy of colonization that is in my ancestry, but that I could work with him to ground and connect to the energy here. I have been working with him ever since. Every time he comes forward to assist me he shows me the ancient forests that were destroyed by the colonists, and in my meditations with him I honor the indigenous people who lost their lives and culture in the historical unfolding that led to me being here.

You might be wondering why would I want to connect with him if he shows me this violent history? Failing to acknowledge this would be an example of spiritual bypassing—it's important for me to know the truth of what has happened on this land. Only then can I work with him to ground my energy and connect to the land from a place of respect. But he only steps forward when I'm in Canada. I see him in my space, feel his rooting energy, and feel supported by his calm presence and strength.

CALL ON YOUR SPIRIT TEAM FOR ENERGETIC SELF SOVEREIGNTY

You can bring forward your Spirit Team to help you practice Energetic Self Sovereignty any time you feel you need extra support and shielding. To recap, Energetic Self Sovereignty is a practice to help you to be fully in your own energy and to remove or block energy from others from entering your energetic intuitive body.

Calling on your Spirit Team is as simple as asking for them to step forward to help you ground and shield your energy. Either say out loud or in your head: *"Spirit Team, I call on you to shield my energy. Please step forward to support me and guide me."* Or whatever words feel good for you. I like to visualize their energy stepping forward and entering into my energy body. Always set the intention that you are calling forward a benevolent energy. As we said in Chapter 3 you have a choice on who you call forward.

Some times to get into a regular practice with this include: before going to bed; going to a party or other group gathering; before you start a guided meditation and open up your energetic intuitive body to receive messages; going into work or busy public places. Or any time when you are feeling anxious, sensitive and uncertain about what is presenting in your life.

You can also ask your Spirit Team to guard the energy of a specific room in your house or even your entire home. You can do this if you're not feeling safe in a certain space, feel energetically threatened by a person, or feel the negative energy of a spirit you don't want in your space. To do this, simply call on your Team and imagine them shielding the room in question, or the whole of your home, including your garden if you have one, your front door, and all the windows.

It can also be helpful to ask for their protection when you do the Grounding Forcefield Visualisation, shared on page 52. Calling on your Team when you do a meditation or visualization not only asks for their energetic support, but you're also inviting them in to share intuitive guidance with you in that moment.

YOUR LOVED ONE GUIDES

Family members, friends and even pets who have crossed to the other side are also part of your Spirit Team. When we think about connecting with deceased loved ones, we often think of Mediumship, which is the New Age description of this practice. This may bring up images of stereotypical seances, rituals to call on the dead, or a TV psychic, saying, "I have someone here with a name that starts with T!" But the truth is, we are all "mediums." As with all intuitive tools, some people are naturally stronger in this area, but you don't need a special gift to be able to connect and communicate with the energy of these beings. We can get practical guidance from them, as well as emotional support as they remind us of key memories that brought us joy and laughter. I love when I can feel the energy of my childhood dog around me, it feels like I'm getting a big hug.

Of course, for many of us there are people in our family who have passed whose energy we would not want to connect with. This may include anybody who caused us personal trauma, or certain family members who may have instigated harm, upset or drama in our wider family constellation. Rather than feeling that they are there to support and guide us, we may even feel that we want to shield our energy from them. This is completely understandable, and it's important to remember that it is ALWAYS your personal choice to decide to work with or call upon a particular individual. If they show up uninvited and you don't want to connect with them you can ask them to leave. If this happens when you're having a session with a professional reader, you can always decline to hear the message that is coming through.

But if a loved one who has caused harm to you or the family comes through and you get a "Hell Yes" that you should interact with them, practice discernment and ask them what they would like to share. Remember: YOU ARE IN CHARGE.

When you call on a Loved One Guide, you'll know when they are around because their energetic presence will feel the same as when they were alive. Whether it's your Grandmother, a friend, or a beloved pet, you might even notice the scent of their clothes, their perfume or a drink they used to love. For example, every time my Grandmother is around I can smell her favorite brand of cigarettes! If your Intuitive Seeing is strong, and you see a Loved One Guide, be aware that they sometimes don't show up at the age that they passed over. They can also show up as a younger version of themselves, as if they are reenacting a time from their own past. Especially if they loved that time of their life and had fond memories of it.

As mentioned, they can also show up uninvited, while you may also notice their energy around you at certain times of the year, such as birthdays, anniversaries, or certain times of the year you always spent together.

Likewise, if you visit a place they loved, had a personal history with, or had fond memories of, you may feel their presence more strongly. You can also call upon them by holding an object or piece of clothing that belonged to them, or by calling forward a special memory you had with them.

One question I am often asked on this topic is, "How can I connect to a loved one who's passed over if their soul has reincarnated into another human body? Does this mean I can never contact them again?" Which is a great question—if someone dies it seems logical that their soul is wiped clean and forgotten as they move into their next life.

But when we connect to a Loved One Guide, we're connecting to the unique energetic imprint of the life in which we knew them. Their personality traits, their memories, and the stories of that life. This imprint is stored in a liminal "in between" space of no time, a bit like the energy of the "empty room" exercise from Chapter 6. When your Loved One Guides show themselves to you they typically show up in peace, and free from any burdens, worries and regrets they may have experienced when they were living. They are no longer in pain, but have "gone home" and are at peace. They are a reminder that we are all energy beings that have chosen this human existence to learn, and when we have completed our "curriculum" we get to go back home to ∞. This means we are connecting to our Loved One's evolved self, or soul, even if they have reincarnated into another body. They can share with us what their learning was from their lifetime, and even what they would have done differently in their life. This can provide us with healing, understanding and closure.

YOUR ANCESTOR GUIDES

Beyond grandparents and great grandparents, the majority of us have no idea who our Ancestors were as their stories get lost over time. These ancient relatives are in our Team not only to guide us, but to support us to right the wrongs of their past, so that we don't repeat their mistakes. Their energy is like a thread that connects us all together through time and space. When working with Ancestors, rather than visualizing and calling on a specific "person" for support, it's about connecting to the collective universal energy of your ancestral lineage. This means all the women and men that came before you, and who played their roles in the creation of your entire family tree. All of whom experienced their own life struggles and challenges as part of the evolution of this planet, and who are here to guide you on your journey.

Many of us do not feel connected to our ancestry, or even relate to what we do know about our ancestors in a positive way. Whether we identify as Black, Indigenous, People of Color (BIPOC) or are white, we have a shared history of persecution and oppression through slavery and colonialism, where the white ancestor was the oppressor and the BIPOC ancestor was the oppressed. While further from living memory, women of European descent also carry the ancestral wounds of the witch hunts, when millions were murdered at the hands of the patriarchy. This past is part of the ancestral energy we continue to connect to and, unfortunately, is still part of our society today—and while acknowledging these wounds, it is essential for white descendants to continue to look at how they may unconsciously or inherently be engaged in harmful behavior to BIPOC-bodied people today. (More coming up in the final three chapters of the book on why it is more important than ever for us to confront this head-on).

So how do we hold all of this when thinking about our ancestral roots? When our Ancestors step forward they're asking us to create change. They're supporting us so we can heal from their past actions, whether this is the harm they caused, or the harm that was done to them. They too show up in their "evolved" state, holding the vision of hope so we can heal as a collective. But this isn't about forgetting past traumas and pretending they didn't happen—in contrast, they must be fully acknowledged before we can move on. In this way, our Ancestor Guides can help us to remember, and to learn. But as with Loved Ones Guides if there is part of your ancestry you do not wish to invite in you have a choice. Just be aware of whether your unwillingness to connect with them comes from a fear of facing their truths.

If you don't know much about your ancestral lineage, and you want to deepen the connection to this part of your story, you can take some time to research where your ancestors came from, what their lives were like, and what challenges they may have faced. There's a whole section coming up on how to work with the stories of your ancestors to help heal you and connect you to your inner truth. This research can strengthen your energetic connection to them, so you can receive their wisdom and intuitive guidance.

This brings a whole other dimension to working with ancestral energy, as we get to see our life as part of the collective planetary ancestral lineage. This collective ancestral energy is made up of all the Indigenous knowledge of all races and all spiritual traditions that have ever walked this planet. During times of global chaos, uncertainty, and transformation, we are all being called to attune to this energy—in ways that can often feel confronting when we are pulled into it unconsciously. It can make us feel emotional, triggered, defensive or over-sensitive and wonder why this is happening. But we can consciously connect to our collective ancestor story by not hiding the truths of the past, by being honest with ourselves about what is unfolding, and by taking action to create change. As we embrace this part of our intuitive power, we find we can take strength from the supportive energy of our ancestors, as we are also reminded not to repeat the same mistakes and injustices of the past.

YOUR ANCESTOR ALTAR

You can create a sacred space to connect with your Ancestor Guides and work with their energy. This doesn't need to be anything elaborate, the point is to have a special space to honor their energy, their traditions, and their history.

You can dedicate a certain area in your home to your Ancestor Altar, like a windowsill, the top of a dresser, or a specific space on a bookshelf. You could include photographs of your ancestors (if they're available to you), a copy of an ancestral story or myth, a piece of art or creative expression, map of where they're from, or a candle. If you know of a spiritual tradition or ritual that's connected to your lineage, you can use this space to honor this practice. You could also include an object or piece of jewelry connected to your ancestral lineage, or a written list of the names of ancestors your research has brought up. But your Ancestor Altar can also be as simple as a vase of flowers that you dedicate each week to the souls that make up your lineage. A meal that you cook in honor of them. A movement practice that you dedicate to them. Or a prayer thanking them for being part of your Spirit Team. Remember you don't need to know all the details to honor them.

HOW TO WORK WITH YOUR SPIRIT TEAM

Now that you've met the different members of your Spirit Team, let's take a closer look at how to work with them. We can call on them whenever we get an intuitive hit to ask for their assistance, which could be any time we're looking for guidance, asking for a sign, or would like to feel more supported. They can help with specific answers, and their presence can simply help us feel more calm, anchored, and grounded in our bodies. Any time we're feeling uncertain or anxious about a personal experience or something that is happening in the collective, it can be incredibly helpful just to know they are there.

But as with all ways of connecting to your intuitive power, trust is vital. This means trusting that they are there for us unconditionally, even when we can't "feel" their presence, and we still seem to be grasping in the dark for answers. The truth is, sometimes our Team will step back to *allow* us to feel uncomfortable in the not knowing. To encourage us to surrender into the uncertainty. Like a loving parent sending their child away to camp for the first time, in these moments members of our Spirit Team are asking us to lean even deeper into trusting our own inner truths.

Our Spirit Team will also show up in ways that are unique to us. As this team is part of our intuitive power, we all connect to them in our own ways, the same as with all of our gifts. As you practice working and interacting with them, you will discover your own language for communicating with them.

This will happen as you engage with your Intuitive gifts of Seeing, Hearing, Feeling, and Knowing. For example, you may Feel their presence around you, or simply Know when they are communicating with you.

With Intuitive Hearing specifically, you may actually hear their voice in your head. But more often than not, you will hear your own voice accompanied by a feeling of their energy.

With Intuitive Seeing, we all have the potential to see our Spirit Team, as well as other spirits who aren't part of our team, and the "ghosts" of people we personally don't know who have passed—the same way that my main Guide appeared to me as an orb of icy blue light. But you will never see them as "real" solid people in your space. They are more likely to appear like a hologram, or as a projection into the world around you. You may also see them in your mind, as you saw objects in the "Empty Room" exercise for Intuitive Seeing.

It's also important to know that you don't have to know every detail about who is on your Spirit Team to connect with them, or know that they are there. It's nice to know what they look like and where they're from, but this makes little difference to their capacity to offer you guidance, support and energetic shielding. Your job is to learn to trust that they are there, and getting used to calling on them is the most important step. Remember, needing to "get it right" or for your intuition to show up in a certain way is one of the blocks to you accessing your gifts and taking back your power. Give yourself permission not to know, and to simply believe.

◇◇◇◇◇

INTUITIVE ACTION

The following exercises offer practical ways to begin to work with your Spirit Team. If you don't get many details from them at first, go slow and allow them to reveal themselves to you. If you're not feeling a connection to them, be okay with that. As with reactivating all our intuitive gifts, it takes practice and patience to connect with your Spirit Team. Trust that they are there for you, and allow yourself to discover more about them over time.

"What do I need to know today?"

One way to begin to connect is to call on your Team for a specific message.

To do this, simply call on them to step forward. You can put yourself into the Empty Room if you like or simply allow yourself to feel them entering your energetic field. You can also listen to the Spirit Team Empty Room guided meditation (below) to guide you through this process.

When you feel their presence, even if it's only very subtle, begin by asking the question: "What do I need to know today?" And see what comes through. You can also do this in the shower in the morning, or as part of a meditation practice.

You can call on the energy of your whole team to answer or you might pick out your main guide.
Notice what feelings or sensations arise in your body. Notice where your thoughts go and what themes and patterns come up. Notice if you see any symbols, words or imagery. Notice what you know to be true.

Once you have received any messages, thank them for their guidance.

Spirit Team Writing
You can also connect to your Team and receive their guidance through writing. You might have heard this practice referred to as "automatic writing" or "channeled writing"—these are different to journaling as you write not from your normal Ego / Fear Voice, but allow your Team to energetically write through you in your Intuitive Voice.

To try it out, start a brand new page in a diary, journal, or digital note. Begin this process by doing the Grounding Forcefield Visualization, and asking your team to step forward before you start to write. Imagine the Energy Faucet being turned on and flowing onto the page.

As you start to write, you may notice what sounds like your Ego / Fear Voice to begin with. This is because when we first start we're usually writing what we *think* we want to hear or know, and we try to control what we're writing. To let your Spirit Team take over, get out of your head and focus your energy into your heart space.

Imagine your whole intuitive body vibrating and ready to receive guidance. The key is to not overthink and not worry about it being perfect. Trust whatever wants to come through—even (in fact especially!) if it doesn't make sense at first. Remember, intuition has its own logic, and what comes through might surprise you.

If you're struggling to write anything, and feel like you're stuck in your head, you can bring more structure to the process by writing out questions that you'd like answered, or themes in your life you'd like guidance on. For example, "Where in my life am I blocking my heart?" "What should I do about this person?" "What will happen if I follow this career path?"

Signs from your Spirit Team

You can also assign a particular sign to your Spirit Team, so you know when they're around you. For example, there might be an animal, a color, a symbol, a word, or song that you associate with a specific Guide, Ancestor or Loved One. My sign is an owl, and I know when this appears in my life that my Team is letting me know I'm on the right track. It might appear on a T-shirt or a car sticker, someone might mention an owl, or I may even see a real owl.

Members of your Spirit Team may also choose a sign for you, showing it to you on repeat until you understand that this is how you will know when they are around. It will feel like something that's trying to get your attention. For example, I know my ancestors, and my Grandfather specifically, is around, whenever I see an eagle. Or when I see a heron I know it's my Auntie Gill saying "hi." Another one of my Spirit Team signs is the Seven Sisters constellation. When I feel drawn to look up to the night sky and can see this constellation I feel connected to my Starseed guides.

GUIDED MEDITATION

The guided meditation for this chapter is titled "Spirit Team in the Empty

Room." It's designed to help you to connect to the energy of your Guides, Ancestors and Loved Ones, as a start to work with their guidance. You can find it in the online portal.

REPEAT TO INVOKE YOUR SPIRIT TEAM

I call on my Spirit Team

I call you forward

I am here. I am ready

I call on the energy of my spirit guides

I call on the energy of my loved ones

I call on the energy of my ancestors

I call on the energy of the collective ancestors

I call on you to support me and guide me

I call on you to shield me and for Energetic Self-Sovereignty

I call on you so I can feel calm, grounded, and loved

I trust your presence is always here

I am here to receive your wisdom, insight, and healing

I call you forward

9
HEALING THE PRESENT MOMENT

If you're like most people, you probably think of psychics and intuitives as being able to tell the future. And maybe that's why you picked up this book: to discover how to use *your* gifts to work out what's in store for you, so you can live your #bestlife. When things aren't going so great (and even when they are) the temptation can be to turn our focus to the future us, and what we want to happen next. But the only way to get THERE is by healing the NOW in your life. And while it's entirely possible to get intuitive guidance about how your life will play out should you make certain decisions today, healing the present moment is what the gift of intuition is really for.

It is yet more old paradigm thinking that working with your intuition is all about "fortune telling." Yes, you may well get intuitive hits about how a situation will play out, or warning messages of potential threats to watch out for. But focusing on the future is essentially about trying to control outcomes, in an attempt to feel more secure. This gets dialed up when we're living through uncertain times, both on a personal and a collective level. The less certainty there is in the world, the more we begin to obsess about what the future might hold.

But can you see how this is another way we give our power away? Part of us believes that the power lies in the hands of our *future* self, *future* life or in what the future of the collective looks like. This societal programming keeps us playing small, in fear, and disconnected from our truth, *today*. What if we realized that we could access our intuitive power and our gifts right NOW—and in doing so, shape the future we desire. By using our intuition to heal the present moment we are taking back our power TODAY.

Of course, imagining possible future outcomes can give us hope and help us find a new direction to follow, but it's also part of our societal conditioning to always be looking ahead, instead of appreciating where we're at. Whether it's focusing on what we want *next* in our career, wondering if we're in the right relationship, or planning a vacation, the message is always the same: there's always something "better" than what you have right now. But the truth is that only in the here and now do we have access to our full agency over how the future actually plays out.

Ultimately, connecting to our intuitive power is a reconnection with the Self. A recovery of lost or forgotten parts of the whole person that we are, through the use of signs, symbols, patterns and themes. When applied to our day-to-day lives, our intuition helps us make choices that are aligned with the whole person that we are, instead of us being influenced by beliefs that have been imprinted by past traumas, ancestral inheritances, and societal conditioning.

In this chapter, I'm going to show you how to use your intuitive power to heal yourself, right here and right now. In this, you will begin to course correct and clear a new path towards meeting the future self you know you are here to be.

MY JOURNEY TO REVEAL INTUITION
IN THE PRESENT MOMENT

After my own spiritual reactivation I realized that I was being presented with an opportunity to do some deep shadow work and look at all the parts of me that needed to be healed. As I was lying in the bath one evening, I received an intuitive message that simply said: *"I choose me."* I got full body goosebumps and ∞ kept repeating the message. This led me to notice the themes and patterns through my life where I could see I'd been waiting to be "chosen" by others all my life—whether in my work, my passions, my romantic relationships, or my family life. For me, healing the present moment meant looking at why this was. I began to learn that I'd grown up believing that the power was outside of myself. That my opportunities to receive love, create success and happiness were dependent on others versus me believing in my own power and choosing myself. I decided that this wasn't how I wanted to live my life any more and decided to follow what brought me joy in the NOW instead.

This led to my decision to create a business based on my intuitive gifts, and start offering client sessions. But despite using my intuition very differently in my own life, I was still hooked into this work being about seeing into the future. I'd been conditioned that the only reason people would want to see a "psychic" was so that I could tell them what would happen next in their life, and that my success lay in the accuracy of my predictions.

Over time however, my Spirit Team made it very clear that this was not the purpose of my work. My sessions shifted dramatically from making predictions, to looking at what was happening in the present moment, and how this was connected to unhealed traumas of the past. When working with a client, ∞ would show me what was happening in their life right now, why it was happening, and how this often had its roots all the way back in their childhood, where the first seeds of doubt and fear were planted in a person's physical, emotional and energetic bodies.

For example, I might receive a message that showed me how a childhood friend moving to a different city created a sense of abandonment that remained imprinted in a client's energy body. Or how a past heartbreak had led to them putting a wall around their heart, leading to trouble opening up to love today. This process allowed them to heal and release these moments as they realized how the past was still impacting them in the now. Many of my clients have described the sessions as being like "therapy." But that it felt even more magical when the guidance they received came from ∞, or was being shared by an intuitive who didn't know any of their past history.

But I could also see that being the "messenger" created an attachment to me in my clients. As if they could only thrive and move forward from a place of power when receiving my guidance. I began to consider how I could empower others to be able to use their own intuitive gifts so that they could bring the same insights that I was able to give them to their own daily trials and traumas.

This solidified a few years after I started my practice, after I received an email from a client I'd seen when I first started working as a professional intuitive. They wanted to let me know they were pissed off, because life hadn't turned out the way I'd predicted. At first, I was upset that my reading hadn't been "accurate," and that they were disappointed. I could tell from their tone they weren't happy in their life. But I was also amazed at the extent to which they'd clung to my predictions. As if no other outcome could possibly be "right" for them.

So I tuned into ∞ and asked: "What is the learning for me here? What am I to take from this?" The message was clear: *"This is to show you that your mission is to help others connect with their own intuitive power. To show them that this is a way for them to heal. If we can't heal the present moment and make peace with the past, we will always be disappointed by our future. Because when it arrives we will still be holding our trauma and living from our limiting beliefs, and this will continue to impact our relationships and how we see the world."*

This message came at a time where I was looking for guidance on my "why." I was at a crossroads and wanted more clarity on my purpose. Ironically, the message I needed to help me in the present moment arrived in an email all about telling the future! In this exchange, ∞ also reminded me that we always have free will over any intuitive message or piece of guidance we receive. Whether we take action on it is our choice; a choice that will invariably have an impact on how our future plays out. This showed me that the only way to help somebody live the *future* life they wanted was to empower them to take action on the intuitive guidance they were receiving *today*.

I've since had multiple clients who've come back for repeat sessions, who have asked, *"Why hasn't this part of my life changed? When will this stop happening to me?"* Now, I know that my work is always to help them refocus on where ∞ is asking them to take intuitive action in their life today.

This happened with one client whose love life kept blowing up, as she kept attracting the same type of person over and over again. She felt like whatever she did, nothing changed. But once she realized her work was to focus on what she needed to look at in her life *today*, she was finally able to find her self-worth in her relationships. She looked at where she'd lost her self esteem in all of her past relationships, where she'd stepped out of her power and how this had come about. Rather than focusing on when the "right person" would finally come into her life, she saw that she had been the missing piece all along. She even said to me: "I get it now ... the change I was looking for had to begin with me."

IT'S ALL IN THE ASK

Switching out of future-tripping mode into using intuition for self-healing is easier said than done, and the key lies in *how* you ask questions when accessing your own intuition. Whether you're calling forward your Spirit Team, working with tools (tarot, oracle cards, pendulum, runes), or are simply asking ∞ for guidance, there are specific ways to ask for a message to help you heal the present moment.

First, let's look at some questions to *avoid* or use very sparingly. If you find yourself using the below kind of language when accessing your intuition, pause and ask yourself: *"why do I need to know how things will turn out? What is happening in the present that I am trying to control?"*

What does my future look like?
When will I feel better?
Will my family be okay?
When will I find a partner?
Will I ever get the job I want?
How will I know when I'm on the right path?

Can you already feel the anxiety in this kind of language? Behind each of these questions there is fear, doubt, and a sense of things not being okay. Perhaps there's a tinge of panic about missing out, or pressure to succeed. Read through these questions again, either out loud or in your head. How do they make you feel in your body?

Make a mental note of any sensations that are present, or journal on this for a minute. Notice the impact on your subtle intuitive body when this future-tripping language takes you out of the present moment. Now let's switch up the energy, and reframe these questions to help you heal the present moment. If you feel called, you can use these questions as journal prompts and for automatic or channeled writing.

What do I need to know today?
What is holding me back right now?
Who can support me on my journey?
How am I blocking myself?
What is this situation here to teach me?
What does success look like to me?

Notice how this language creates new pathways into your physical, emotional and energetic bodies. Can you feel how much more powerful this is? Questions like these allow ∞ to show you the information available to you right now. This in turn creates an opening for whatever future possibilities (of which there are always many) want to come through for you.

Read these questions again, either out loud or in your head. How do they make you feel in your body? Again, make a mental note of this, or write anything down you feel called to.

Many people find that re-framing their questions in this way brings a sense of calm, and helps them feel more in control over a current life situation. This is because you're asking for guidance you can use and act on RIGHT NOW, versus giving your power to an imaginary future self. When we're feeling desperate, confused, angry, or fearful, our first instinct can be to want to escape from the present. But taking back control of your life and your power, begins with looking at what the present moment is trying to show you. Asking ∞ to help you uncover what's really happening right now, and moreso how this is connected to the past, is where you will find everything you need to help you move forward.

USING YOUR DREAMS TO HEAL

Our dreams are another place we can access intuitive guidance to heal the present moment, especially when we feel blocked, confused, or anxious about how the future will play out. Whether you remember your dreams or not, they act as a visual metaphor for the workings of our psyche. Often full of sensory messages that are ripe for intuitive interpretation, they are another way our energetic intuitive body shares wisdom and guidance with us. Dreams can provide deep insight into fears, blocks, desires, and anxieties we may not even be connected to in our waking life, but which are pulling levers and influencing our actions from behind the scenes.

Signs that a dream contains an intuitive message for you are recurring dreams, special places we like to return to in our dreams, or dreams where we travel to other worlds and dimensions. Some people also experience lucid dreaming, where they are able to control the dream narrative. If you're a lucid dreamer then this is part of your intuitive gifts, as you can ask for guidance within your dream state.

Have you ever experienced déjà vu, where you do something and it feels like it's happened before? It can feel super strange, like a glitch in the matrix, and you might even ask yourself, *"Have I dreamt this already?"* If this happens to you, trust that this might actually be true. Déjà vu can also be an intuitive marker, or visual sign, that you're on the right path. Any time you experience it, pause and ask yourself: *"Why is this moment trying to get my attention? What is my learning right now? What is it trying to show me?"*

Others experience prophetic dreams, where they are shown an intuitive vision of something that is yet to pass—and which is only revealed as such when the events of the dream "come true" in waking life. This can be overwhelming the first time it happens, as it shows you the power of your dreamscape.

Of course, many of us don't remember our dreams at all, and if we do it's only in fragments. In which case, how are you supposed to use them to get intuitive messages about what's happening in your life? Firstly, please don't see this as another skill to "master." Whether you're a regular dreamer or someone who only remembers the occasional dream, simply allow your dreams to be another avenue to explore in your wider intuition practice. If you feel called, the practices below are a way to have a play with this, without any pressure of "getting something."

INTUITIVE DREAM PRACTICES

Spirit Dream Team

Before you sleep, set the intention that you want to remember your dreams. You can simply say out loud or in your head: "I would like to remember my dreams in the morning." You can also call on your Spirit Team at this time and ask them to interact with you in your dreams. Or call on a specific loved one, Ancestor or Spirit Guide. You may also meet new members of your Spirit Team as you dream. If you're someone that suffers from nightmares or sleep paralysis, you can also ask for them to shield you in your sleep (follow the Grounding Forcefield Visualization technique that's in Chapter 3 on page 52).

Dream Journal

One of the easiest ways to start working with your dreams is to start writing down whatever you remember from your dreams. Keep a specific dream journal and pen by your bed, so you can literally roll over and jot down any memories on waking before your dream disappears. Sometimes just writing one word will trigger a memory about the rest of the dream, as well as give you a clue to its meaning. With practice you'll be able to recall more of your dreams in detail.

Dream Themes

By keeping a journal you'll be able to notice what themes, patterns and symbols keep coming up in your dreams. As with decoding your intuitive messages, pause and ask yourself: *What do these symbols and themes mean to me? What part of my life does this relate to?* Also note down how you felt in your body when you woke from the dream. Did you wake from the dream feeling sad, angry, deflated, excited or aroused? This can give you a good indication of what your intuitive body is trying to communicate in the dream. It's all part of the message.

Ask a Question

Using the list of "present moment" questions above, select a question you would like more clarity on before you sleep. Call on your Spirit Team and ask to be shown an answer in your dream state. You might receive the answer over more than one night's sleep. So make a note of what came through each morning, and reflect on how it fits the question until you feel you have enough clarity.

Plants for Dreaming
Certain plants have the power to connect us more deeply to our dreams, and help us get into a more lucid dream state. Blue lotus, which was sacred to the Egyptians, or Mugwort are two options. Always endeavor to use wildcrafted or ethically sourced plants.

If you're looking for some additional dream support, you could also go to a dream interpreter or dream shaman to help you unlock the messages of your dreamstate. But have a go at decoding what they mean to you first before asking for the support of someone else.

HEALING YOUR ANCESTOR STORY

In the last chapter we discovered how your ancestors are part of your Spirit Team and how you can connect with them. And your relationship to your "Ancestor Story" has its own important role to play in helping you take back your power in the here and now.

Our Ancestor Story is my term for the web of themes, patterns, blocks, and beliefs we have inherited from our ancestors—both our ancestry going back hundreds of years, and also our immediate lineage: parents, grandparents, and great-grandparents. While we often sense this on an intuitive level, even science confirms it, with epigenetics (which is the study of our genes and DNA) showing how we carry the trauma of our ancestors in our DNA. And while this impacts everything about the lives we are living today, often these themes are passed on from generation to generation without us even realizing. Let's look at what makes working with our Ancestor Story such a vital piece in our healing today.

As I began to focus more on getting information on what was happening RIGHT NOW in my one-on-one client sessions, ∞ would regularly share that the blocks they were experiencing were inherited from previous generations. For example feeling unloved in relationships, always being in a caregiver/provider role, or having issues with money. This in turn showed me that it was vital for my clients to address these past patterns, or they would remain stuck in the same cycles on repeat, unable to move forward and create the future outcomes they desired.

But time isn't linear, and the threads of our Ancestor Story travel from the past, to the present and into the future. This means that when we identify, heal, and release Ancestor Story patterns in the present moment, we're also healing trauma on behalf of past generations and the future generations yet to come. Can you already feel how freeing this has the potential to be? But also how it might be very deep, and painful to go on this ancestor journey. To bring up past traumas in your own life, in your family, and to be present with the systemic trauma we face as a collective, isn't easy. When we begin this process, it's important to remember that we are in charge, so we can go at our own pace and stop any time it becomes too much. We can also call on the support of a therapist or other healer as we work through this.

Any of us can begin this healing process at any time, regardless of our connection to our lineage and ancestry. Maybe you don't know much about your family history, are adopted, or simply don't relate to what you know about your ancestors. All it takes is an awareness of the blocks stemming from your Ancestor Story and an intention to heal them, and to allow the energy of your Ancestor Story into your energetic intuitive body so you can see how it's impacting you today. In client sessions, it's also come through that people who have been adopted can carry the stories of both their birth and adoptive families, which shows that our Ancestor Story is as much about our upbringing and our conditioning as it is about our bloodline.

Looking at our Ancestor Story can give us clarity on why we have regular feelings of being abandoned or alone, of being unable to give or receive love, or of having repetitive drama surrounding money or career. It can also shine a light on issues around belonging, being seen, and a lack of self-worth, as well as blocks to physical or emotional intimacy, and issues with trust, control, and personal freedom.

There's so much hidden in our Ancestor Stories, I could write a whole book on this subject. The process is a blend of fact finding, intuitive led guided meditations, creative imagination, and journaling, and can help us understand not just our familial relationships, but our relationship to money, our health, our career, and to love. The process can take years and once you start to identify your Ancestor Story, you'll always be seeing new patterns and aspects that are part of the web. But here are some first steps for beginning to work on them in the here and now.

THE ANCESTOR WEB

The first part of the process is to consider what you do know about your ancestors, beginning with your family history. What do you know about the challenges your parents faced? How about your grandparents, and your great-grandparents? If you have a relationship with them, reach out to living relatives and ask about their childhood, their upbringing, where they lived. Find out about the work they did, and what dreams they had for themselves. If it feels right you can even ask them: "What did you feel you were trying to overcome in your life?" "How were your relationships" or "What has been your biggest life learning?" Their answers to questions like these will give clues as to the themes of your lineage.

You can do this for the maternal and paternal lines of the family, your caregivers or members of your adopted family. If the people you'd like to hear from aren't alive anymore but you know someone who had a connection to them (a family friend for example) you can try seeing what they have to say.

Part of the journey is also to look to our older ancestors, and their role in the collective traumas of the planet. For example, for BIPOC identifying people, what is your relationship to your history? Including the history of your land, ancestors, and their relationship to the land (reciprocity). How might this have changed since your great

great parents' time? Where may you be willing or ready to unpack historical trauma in your family and with whom? What providers, healers or helping professionals can hold space for your work? If you're a white person of European descent, what was your ancestors' role in colonialism? How might they have been impacted by the witch trials? What privileges and/or traumas are you still experiencing today as a result?

It's amazing what can come through in these investigations. So often our ancestors haven't been given the opportunity to tell the stories they have lived, and we live in a culture in the West where very little importance is placed on our shared histories with our family of origin. This is a loss, but we can begin to reclaim it any time we choose.

Your Part in the Web
The next step is to discover your place in your lineage, or Ancestor Web. Read through the below questions and take your time to journal on what comes up for you.

What was your childhood like?
What happened back then that has shaped who you are today?
What was the emotional tone of your home growing up?
Did you have freedom or were you raised in a strict household with lots of rules?
How was your health?
Did you feel safe?
What made you feel worthy?
Did you move around a lot as a child?
What adversities or struggles did you face as a family?
What values were instilled in you?
What were your hopes and dreams for the future?

Write down anything that comes up for you, including any key moments and memories, and know you can stop at any point if it becomes too triggering for you. You're the one in charge of bringing up the events, emotions, and feelings you remember from this time.

If there's a particular area you feel blocked in, you can repeat the exercise with a specific focus on your friendships, romantic partnerships, money, or career.

Connecting the Dots

Now it's time to notice what themes appear in both the stories of your ancestors and in your own life. What energetic imprints do you think you might have inherited from them? How might these be impacting your life today, and therefore the choices you make that will dictate how your future plays out?

Reflect on a current situation where you feel blocked, confused, or unsure of yourself, and notice if any of your ancestors experienced something similar. For example you may be experiencing problems in your romantic relationships. Looking at how this might be connected to your Ancestor Story, first ask yourself: Am I experiencing codependency? Do I struggle to receive love? Are there trust issues? Do I feel I always have to prove myself in a relationship? Do I settle for people because it feels safe? Has there been manipulation or abuse?

Then look back on what you know of your ancestors' relationships. How did they experience love? It's important to note where the DETAILS might be different (different circumstances, people involved, era etc.) but the THEMES are the same. When we uncover the themes we begin to see the bigger Ancestor Story web and how we're connected to it. You can do this for both sides of your family line and our larger collective Ancestor story.

The more you engage with this process, the more you will notice common themes being repeated—a vital first step in breaking the patterns of the past. From here, the work is to take back your power and act on what your intuition is telling you, versus continuing to play the same old Ancestor Story on repeat. Only by healing the past and its influence on your life today, will you be free to pursue the future that is truly meant for you.

◇◇◇◇◇

Are you beginning to see how powerful it is to focus on healing what's in your life right now? You may have uncovered some patterns in your Ancestor Story that you didn't even realize were running the show behind the scenes of your life, draining your energy and keeping you stuck from moving forwards. The good news is, you get to end these patterns today— and you can use your intuition to do it.

Even better, the healing you begin to enact in your own life will send ripples out into the collective. As if you are literally rewriting history, and, in doing so, reshaping the future we are moving towards together. Seen this way, using your intuition to heal the present moment means bringing your gifts to the world in a bigger way than you probably ever imagined. This is all part of being a Conscious Intuitive, which we are going to talk about in the next chapter.

◇◇◇◇◇

INTUITIVE ACTION

Use the below exercises to begin to use your intuition to heal the present moment.

Ask a NOW question

Pick an area of your life where you'd like some intuitive insight RIGHT NOW. Grab your journal to use the questions below as journal prompts or for channeled writing. Or ask the questions working with your favorite intuitive tool or card deck. You can also come up with your own NOW based question.

What do I need to know today?
What is holding me back right now?
How can I open my heart to receive?
Who can support me on my journey?
How am I blocking myself?
What is this situation here to teach me?
What does a successful outcome look like to me?

Commit to a Dream Practice

Place your journal and pen by your bed and commit to a dream journal practice. On waking, jot down as much as you can remember about your dream—including images, feelings, and overall themes. It might be as little as one word, or a full, cinematic, story. Commit to doing this every morning for one week and see what comes up. Using the practices from the Decoding Your Messages chapter, what are your dreams trying to communicate with you?

Healing dreams in the Awake State

Your Dream Practice might have shown you some repeating patterns and themes—and you can heal these in an awake state by rewriting the story of the dream, and changing the outcome or ending. This can be especially healing if you experience nightmares.

Pick a dream that stands out that you'd like to heal. Ask yourself: *"What do the symbols and themes in the dream mean to me? What part of my life does this relate to?"*

Once you have identified these, write the dream out again, and consciously change the parts of the dream you feel need healing. For example, if you dream that you've lost your passport (which could be a message that you're struggling with your identity), write out a version of the dream where you find it, and feel safe and secure about who you are. Doing this will help bring closure to the theme the dream is showing you.

Your Ancestor Story

Uncovering your Ancestor Story is not a linear A-Z process. If you're feeling overwhelmed, you can start by writing out a list of places you currently feel blocked in your life. Be as specific and as detailed as you can, and include any repetitive blocks that have appeared over the past few years.

These might be around love, money, relationships, health, family, career or home.

Or it might mean looking at repetitive emotions you've been experiencing such as anger, fear, anxiety, worry, love, pleasure and seeing what areas of your life the emotions correlate to.

From here, you can work with them one at a time to see how they may be connected to what you know of or can discover about your ancestors. *Remember that although the DETAILS may be different the THEMES will be the same.*

GUIDED MEDITATION

The guided meditation for this chapter is on "Intuition to Heal the Present Moment" and it will help you drop into your energetic intuitive body and identify the healing that's available to you RIGHT NOW—instead of projecting your energy into the future. You can find it in the online portal.

REPEAT TO INVOKE HEALING IN THE PRESENT MOMENT

I am here

I am present

I am healing

I call on the energy of this moment to help guide me

I am a dreamer

I open the portals to my dreamscape

I unveil the truth of my dreams

I call upon my Spirit Team to help me to remember my dreams

I am part of the Ancestor web

I am ready for my Ancestor Story to be revealed

I am open to see the patterns and themes in the now

I call upon my Ancestors to help me heal our story

I am here

I am present

I am healing

∞

10

BEING A CONSCIOUS INTUITIVE

Connecting with your gifts authentically, in truth, and in honor of the energy you're working with is a vital part of using your intuition the *Now Age* way. This means having an awareness of your intuitive body as a sacred vessel to receive this guidance. Unfortunately, just as there are abuses of power in other areas of our world and lives, this also shows up when it comes to interactions with ∞. As with anything in life, how we use our gifts is up to us. We can choose to use them for manipulation, personal gain, and to do harm to others. Or we can tune in with integrity, love, and compassion.

Remember, your intuition is a tool to help you transform, learn, grow, and evolve, so that you can live fully in your truth—and take back your power in a world that consistently challenges our freedom to be ourselves. But "power" is an interesting word. As much as being in our power gives us agency over how our lives play out, this can easily tip into wanting to control each and every element of our world. Including the other people in it. Which is not to suggest that now you have access to your intuition, you're going to use your gifts to go around dominating people and demanding that you get your way! But it's amazing how much a desire to "help" others or to "fix" a problem can manifest in subtle manipulation tactics.

This is actually rife in the modern spirituality space, which has bloomed into a mainstream, multi-billion dollar industry. When you go through your Spiritual Reactivation it can feel overwhelming—as if you've woken up in a brand new world, where you have so many questions and everybody seems to be selling "the answer." Navigating this space is actually a great way to begin to practice spiritual discernment, and to practice your "Hell Yes" and

"Heck No" responses for who to connect and work with.

For starters, don't take everything at face value. Ask yourself: *"Does this person and their message align with my truth? Does the way they live their life reflect my values? Am I being manipulated by them in any way? What am I being led to believe about myself?"*

Again, there's nothing wrong with people using their gifts professionally and marketing their services. The vast majority of people working in the spiritual space are doing so out of a genuine desire to help. But as you begin to pay more attention, see if you can notice the subtle difference between the bogus, performative ones, and more conscious intuitive practitioners. It's not for me to tell you what resonates with you, and what your values are. This will be different for everyone, and the key is to be in constant communication with your intuition about what feels right for you. But now that you've learned how to connect and work with your intuition, I want to introduce some things to consider to help you become a Conscious Intuitive—whether this is something you want to bring into your professional life, or simply use for yourself.

NO SPIRITUAL BYPASSING

To recap, "spiritual bypassing" refers to using our relationship to the "spiritual" as a way to avoid facing the potentially painful, challenging, or inconvenient truths in ourselves and in the world. It means focusing on "manifesting our dream life" but not looking beneath the surface to see what's really going on, and why we are unhappy or dissatisfied with the life we are living right now.

The first and most important step in becoming a Conscious Intuitive, is to call yourself and others out when things begin to tip into spiritual bypassing mode. You'll know this is happening when you're confronted by a challenging or uncomfortable situation, and your first reaction is to focus on "love and light" or insist on "high vibes only." It might feel like you're inviting more positivity in, but actually this terminology is a way of pulling back from the learning and healing that is being presented to you. Rather than lean into discomfort and use your intuition to look more deeply at what's going on, what feels like the safer or easier option is to push it away or pretend it's not happening.

This also applies when receiving guidance or knowledge from a spiritual teacher, or guru, or in fact anybody who calls themself an "expert" in anything! Ask yourself: *"Is this guidance moving me closer or farther away from my truth? Is this person willing to answer the difficult questions and to confront what's really going on?"*

The truth is, learning how to face your darkness is an essential part of taking back your power—and any "guru" worth their mala beads will encourage this. Rather than pretending your shadow isn't there, they will confirm that it is only by confronting your fears head on that you can see them for what they are. This is how you become the torchbearer, shining the light and warmth of your heart directly onto your fears and lessening their hold on you. And while you may not feel like you're strong enough for this, if something painful keeps coming up through intuitive messages, themes and patterns in your life, trust that you are ready.

An example of this might be facing the painful patterns that keep showing up from your Ancestor Story. Or looking at the root cause of the low self-esteem that leads you to self-sabotage. This level of spiritual integrity also has a ripple effect, not only opening pathways to change and transformation for you, but the collective too. When we decide to work through our shadows as individuals, we are shown how bypassing them actually contributes to and perpetuates the more shadowy, oppressed parts of society.

THERE'S NOTHING TO "FIX"

There's a lot of pressure in the wellness, self-help and spiritual industries to improve or *fix* yourself—the implication in this being that something about you is broken. Instead of helping, this can often have the complete opposite effect, leaving us feeling less confident and connected to ourselves, even as we engage in more and more desperate acts of "self-care." This mindset feeds directly into the patriarchal idea that we should always be DOING something to feel or perform better.

But working with your intuition reminds you that everything you need is already in you. That any time you feel confused, fearful, sad, or alone, the best thing you can "do" is give yourself permission to simply "be." To rest, pause, and notice what message wants to come through to guide you. When you're in a constant state of doing, with no time for being, it's impossible to receive this guidance. If you're stuck in "doing" you may feel scattered energetically and like all your energy is moving in different directions. The Ego / Fear Voice might be telling you that this self help work or practice is what you "should" or "must" be doing.

When you drop into "being" you will feel more anchored into your intuitive body. The Ego / Fear Voice will quieten and you'll discover what you *really* need in each moment. This may be uncomfortable at first, and feel completely counterintuitive to how you normally act. If you're someone who runs away from stillness and fills your day with being busy this will be an ongoing practice for you.

PRACTICING INTUITIVE INTEGRITY

Intuition is a sacred gift that we all have unlimited access to—and it's important to remember that learning how to work with it doesn't make you "special" or "above" anybody else, as if you are now part of some elite club. This mentality just creates more separation and otherness. Intuition is not an "us and them" situation. Every human being on the planet is intuitive, and we are all evolving as a collective.

If you have reached a point where you feel you have begun to master your intuition, you actually have a great responsibility to honor this gift and to practice intuitive integrity. This means noticing any time you or others are using your gifts to have power over others, to create influence, or to try to control the world around you.

Here are some red flags to be aware of:

- **Intuitive Spying**
  As discussed in Chapter 3, practicing Energetic Self-Sovereignty is key

to feeling safe and grounded as you access your intuition. It also helps shield us, so we don't take on other people's energy—a trick that works both ways. It is a massive abuse of power to use your gifts to "invade" other people's energy, even if you're doing it because you want to help them. As tempting as it might be to ask questions on somebody else's behalf, or to use your gifts to discover a truth they may not be able to see, this is essentially "intuitive spying"—and a serious breach of integrity. How would you like it being done to you? Your gifts are not for keeping tabs on other people. *If you feel like this is being done to you go back and read the practices in the Energetic Self-Sovereignty chapter.*

- **Intuitive Consent**
Of course, sometimes it is absolutely okay to provide intuitive guidance for others. Sometimes you may even receive a message for somebody else completely out of the blue. You'll know the difference between this and intentionally spying on someone, and the key is to ask permission before you share it with them. They may not want to hear what you have to say and that's their choice. Think of this a bit like asking for sexual consent. If it's a "no," don't try to persuade them they need to hear it.

- **Intuitive Manipulation**
Your gifts are also not for trying to create a desired outcome in your life or to get others to do something you want. For example, don't try to pretend that your opinion about something is actually an intuitive message: "∞ *told me to tell you that you should really do it this way.*" Even when you think you have a person's best interests at heart, this type of manipulation is all kinds of wrong, as it takes them out of *their* power. The ego can also be really slippery when it wants to stay in control, and may even try to convince you that what you're sharing is a genuine message. How to tell the difference?

The Ego / Fear Voice has an expectation, an agenda, and is looking for a solution. The Intuitive Voice on the other hand will not feel forced or seem logical.

- **Intuitive Harm**

  If someone has pissed you off, you've fallen out with them, or they've caused harm to you or somebody you care about, it may be tempting to send some "negative energy" back their way. You could do this by imagining hooking your energy into their energetic intuitive body to cause harm, or by speaking out loud a negative invocation with the intent to inflict hurt. But this will only come back to bite you. Instead step out of the energy between you and this person. Practice some of the Energetic Self-Sovereignty techniques to cleanse and reset your energy. When you feel ready use your intuitive gifts to "heal the present moment," ask yourself: *Why has this situation come about? What is the learning for me? What boundaries do I need to create? Am I in my truth or is my ego in charge? Which next action can I take that is based in authenticity, integrity and honoring?*

Remember you can also call on your Spirit Team to shield you if you are experiencing your Energetic Self-Sovereignty coming under attack from someone or something.

INTUITION UNDER THE INFLUENCE

You may feel more "open" to ∞ after drinking a couple of glasses of wine or imbibing other perception-altering substances, as if the guidance is flowing so easily you could tap in at the drop of a hat. You may feel more relaxed, more in the flow, and more connected to your "true" self. But are you really? As soon as the substance in question wears off and the hangover or comedown hits, you probably feel less "connected" than ever.

Even though alcohol and other drugs can make us feel like we're more in tune with our intuitive body, what's actually happening is that the ego mind has been put on mute—making it easier to "hear" and trust your intuition. On an energetic level, you are actually escaping and leaving your body behind. While this leaves you ungrounded and takes you out of your Energetic Self-Sovereignty, it can feel so "easy" to connect this way, it can also become addictive. As if you "need" a certain substance to connect to your gifts.

Yes, it might take a little longer and require a little more practice to connect stone, cold, sober, but as we've already discussed, messages will appear when you are ready to receive them. Using alcohol or other drugs to tap in is falling once again into the same trap of instant gratification that has us turning to Google for answers—versus developing our own intuitive language. Coming to rely on this means cheating yourself out of the full experience of learning to harness your intuitive power.

It can also be more tempting to abuse our gifts when we're drunk or high. Who doesn't want to be the intuitive "wowing" people with messages from ∞ at the party?! But in these states, you're no longer in control of what you're calling in. This makes you more vulnerable to attracting negative entities—as I experienced with the psychic attack at my friend's birthday party when I had been drinking and smoking weed. The negative entity decided to enter my energetic intuitive body and cause harm. I was more susceptible because I was no longer fully in my body, leaving gaping holes in my energetic field.

On the flipside, you might find that a side-effect of your spiritual reactivation is feeling called to drink or do drugs less often, or to give them up all together. As you begin to attune with the subtle energies, you will likely become more sensitive to substances, and feel the toxic after-effects more strongly. Instead of the pleasurable buzz and sense of freedom you used to experience, they may leave you feeling heavy and tired, and *less* connected to your intuitive power. You might also find your friendship group changes, along with the places and situations where you relax, unwind, or have fun—especially if you find yourself feeling more sensitive around other people who are drinking or taking drugs (another great opportunity to practice Energetic Self-Sovereignty).

There's no right and wrong to navigating this—but as you open further to your gifts, pay attention to any changes in your relationship to substances. You will "intuitively" know what's right for you. The same goes for taking "plant medicines" such as psilocybin mushrooms ("magic mushrooms") or Ayahuasca as part of the spiritual reactivation process. Do what feels right for you and where you are on your journey. You don't "need" these substances to reactivate your gifts, so don't feel pressured to take them if you don't feel called, or if you're only taking them to "speed up the process." Remember, everyone's journey is different.

THE DANGERS OF SPIRITUAL LABELING

It's never been more trendy to label a brand or business as "Spiritual" or "Intuitive." We're in a time where everybody gets to be their own brand (myself included!)—and with this, there also comes the temptation to trademark "new" healing methods, modalities, products, and services. But nothing about spirituality and intuition is new. These are human tools, available to everybody, free of charge, that have been around since time began. This means Intuition is SACRED. When we engage with it we are connecting to ∞. But as spirituality becomes more and more mainstream, and develops into an even bigger industry, the power of the $$$ potential means the brand often becomes the priority.

As humans, labeling things makes them more accessible, for ourselves and our potential audience. But be aware of the spiritual labeling that is happening across social media platforms and businesses. Practice discernment. Ask yourself, *"does this feel genuine? What does the energy of this brand/person feel like? Is it legit?"* And remember, whenever someone says they have a "new label" to describe ∞, a healing modality, or have discovered a "new" way to work with ∞, it's just that. A new *label*. What we're connecting to comes from the same source.

It's exciting that more people are looking towards intuition and spirituality as an anchor during these shifting times. That more of us are returning to our inner power and connection. Hey, it's why you picked up this book. It's also fantastic to see more people sharing their experiences and their intuitive gifts with the world. But let's not lose sight of the fact that intuitive power and connection to ∞ are the property of the collective, and make it all about the label, the brand and the trademark.

SPIRITUAL APPROPRIATION

The dictionary definition of cultural appropriation is: "the act of adopting elements of an outside, often minority culture, including knowledge, practices, and symbols, without understanding or respecting the original culture and context."

This is actually rife in modern spiritual communities, and being a conscious intuitive means doing your research and becoming aware of how you may be adopting elements and practices from cultures that aren't your own. For example, placing statues of gods and deities that aren't from your lineage on your altar, or using sage or palo santo to "smudge" your home or your body of "bad vibes."

Smudging is an Indigenous practice used for purification during ceremony and prayer. But it's become so appropriated, that the traditional white sage used by Indigenous communities is becoming endangered, with bundles for sale in mainstream stores. While this is detrimental for the environment, the original sanctity of the Indigenous practice is also lost as white colonialist capitalism profits from a practice that has been stolen.

In the US and Canada, Indigenous people have lost their lives to defend this practice, along with other spiritual traditions. It wasn't until 1978 with the passing of the American Indian Religious Freedom Act that the native community was even allowed to practice their own spiritual traditions. In this context, can you see how harmful it is for the descendants of white colonialists to engage with these practices without asking—and even profit from them?

Which is not to say you can't borrow from these traditions respectfully. Ideally, find a way to participate in a cultural exchange where you gain permission to participate and learn from that culture, practice or ritual. And if smudging with sage, for example, is not something that's in your lineage, you can engage with "smoke clearing" using other substances instead (as shared on page 59).

We must also be aware of cultural appropriation in the language used by spiritual communities. For example, the word "woke" is often used as a term for someone who is experiencing their Spiritual Reactivation—as in, somebody who has "woken up" to the true nature of the world and who they are.

But the word "woke" originated in the Black community, and was originally used to describe issues of social and racial justice. As far back as 1962, William Melvin Kelly wrote an article in the New York Times called "If You're Woke You Dig It," detailing how white Americans were appropriating Black people's phrases as their own. More recently, "woke" has been used by the Black Lives Matter movement to highlight the continued oppression of Black communities, calling them to #staywoke and take action on the flawed political and social systems. So using the word "woke" in the wrong context actually harms communities of color, as it bypasses and minimizes the struggles of their oppression.

The word "tribe" is also widely used in spiritual and wellness circles, but this is disrespectful, offensive and culturally appropriative to Indigenous peoples. As is the term "spirit animal," which is also widely appropriated. We should only be using the word when referring to Indigenous tribes—and using words such as team, group, network or collective to describe non-indigenous communities.

If you identify as a white person, it may be triggering to read this. Which is a perfect example of being confronted by a collective shadow. While it might feel easier to brush off accusations of cultural or spiritual appropriation, and send "love and light" to all involved, can you see how this is only perpetuating systems of oppression and injustice?

WHERE DOES IT COME FROM?

Equally as important as considering the lineages of the rituals and practices we engage with to connect with our intuition, is the provenance of any "tools" we pick up along the way: crystals, plants, herbs, oracle decks, tinctures, and energy clearing sprays to name a few.

Some important questions to ask yourself might be:

Where were these crystals mined or sourced from?
Were they ethically sourced?
Are they even real? (Yes, there are a LOT of fake crystals out there, just like fake Gucci handbags!)

Are you using local wildcrafted plants and herbs?

Are you buying from a reputable source?

Could I buy from a local, independent supplier, versus one of the big corporations?

Never has it been more evident that we each have a responsibility to Mother Earth. The same way we care about the provenance of our food, clothes, and other products, this means being super aware of the sustainability and environmental imprint of our intuition practice.

INTUITIVE SOCIAL MEDIA

Whether or not you have a spiritual "business," the pressure to be on social media and to create a "platform" is REAL. Because it's what gets the most engagement, and because engagement is what fuels the business model of social media, we're encouraged to use our platforms to share our deepest feelings and emotions with the world on a daily basis. If this wasn't overwhelming enough, we've also been conditioned that if we don't post regularly, up to two times a day, then what we say will get lost in the algorithm—playing directly into our ego's deepest fears: that we will not be liked, validated, seen, or heard by others.

Can you see what's wrong with this picture? As much as social media is a beautiful way to connect with like-minded people, to grow a business, and to have a creative outlet, it has been specifically designed to be as "addictive" as possible. The more we post and comment, the more of our attention and energy can be packaged up and sold to advertisers using social media to showcase their wares. Which doesn't sound very intuitive, does it?!

Think about it: why would you want to share anything with the world unless you genuinely have something to say? Because your Ego / Fear Voice is telling you that you will be left behind and forgotten about unless you play the game.

Given all of this, is "intuitive" social media even possible? The answer is "yes"—if you are a Conscious Intuitive. We already discussed the importance of practicing Energetic Self-Sovereignty on social media, and being aware of the information you are consuming. And the same way everything is made of energy, everything we post on social media has its own energetic frequency. On top of this, we are contributing to the collective consciousness with every post, tweet, share or video we put out into the world. Which means we also need to be super conscious about what we're putting out there, and why.

If we are just posting to "get more" likes and follows, we are also continuing to the energy that some people are "better" or more important than others. What if instead of trying to grow our following, we consciously committed to only posting or commenting on things we genuinely cared about? Whether it be supporting the people you love, or sharing the topics that move you, or the ideas that have been helping you to learn and change your perspectives? This shift would ripple outwards, helping create a more equitable conversation in the collective.

Imagine if there were no follower or like counts on your posts. What would you share then? It takes practice to detach from the ego-centric energy of social media, but posting from a place of conscious intuition also makes it less about external validation, and, over time, will help connect more deeply with the message you *really* want to put out into the world.

THE SPIRITUAL ECHO CHAMBER

The other thing about social media, is that it shows us more and more of what we already "like"—when part of being a Conscious Intuitive is uncovering more about what we don't already know, and seeing ourselves and the world with new eyes. This is so important as we commit to seeing the shadow in ourselves, in our communities, and the collective. We're here to be part of the change, so it's important we step out of the spiritual echo chamber.

It makes sense for us to be drawn to viewpoints that mirror our own, as this helps us feel safe, validated, and like we're part of the gang. But if we're not careful, this can lead to us existing in a spiritual bubble—and yet more spiritual bypassing. When we choose to only see the "light and love" or people who share the same views as us, we are ignoring the reality of what all people are actually experiencing on our planet right now.

To avoid this, notice when you're just feeding yourself the same information from the same old sources. Challenge yourself to get out of your comfort zone, and research different points of view. When we listen to other voices and other people's truths, this in turn helps us to relearn what we thought to be true and we gain stronger clarity on what our personal views actually are—versus the group consensus we are fed. You will begin to see the shadow of what is actually happening in our world and will be able to use your intuition to discover what your role is within this.

◇◇◇◇◇

Ultimately, cultivating conscious intuition means understanding that we are each a unique expression of the collective energy of the planet, and that while we live as individuals, we can impact and be impacted by the energy of the whole. When we are embodying and living as a Conscious Intuitive—meaning using our intuition to live in authenticity, integrity and in honor of our values—we are sending ripples of this energy through our personal lives, and out into the collective. This in turn helps to support and create positive evolution and change.

As we reawaken to the true nature of our intuitive gifts, we realize our responsibility to the traditions of our ancestors, to the planet we live on, and to honoring the differences and similarities between all beings. In the final chapter, we're going to look more closely at how we can use our intuition to have a positive impact on the collective, and why this is needed now more than ever as we navigate these uncertain and transformative times.

◇◇◇◇◇

INTUITIVE ACTION
Use the below exercises to practice being a Conscious Intuitive.

Call on the Dogs
If you need some extra shielding, or if you feel your Energetic Self-Sov-

ereignty is being compromised in any way, you can call on your pack of energetic guard dogs to help you.

To do this, literally visualize a pack of dogs. You may see three, you may see ten. It's all good. Feel their energy and know that they are loyal and will always protect you. Now that you have connected with them, you can call on them any time you like to shield your energy. For example, you can put them at the end of your bed before you sleep, when you're in a situation that feels uncomfortable, or you have a feeling someone is trying to connect with your energy without permission.

Alcohol & Drugs

If you drink or use other drugs, notice what happens to your intuitive gifts next time you imbibe. This will help you to see the impact of these substances on your energetic intuitive body. Ask yourself:

Do you feel more in tune with your gifts?
How do you feel energetically in your body?
Do you feel more in control or less in control?
How did you feel afterwards when their effects have worn off?

Again, there's no right or wrong, this is about working out what works for you.

Sustainable Crystal or Plant Energy

You don't always have to "buy" crystals or plants for them to be part of your intuitive practice—you can simply create a visual of them in your imagination to call on their energy.

Firstly, if you feel called, go online and research what the crystal or plant you're interested in working with looks like. This isn't necessary but can help you to connect. Always go with what you're intuitively being drawn to. It might not make sense, but it will feel right.

Next, simply close your eyes and say out loud or in your head: *"I call on the energy of [enter name of crystal or plant]"* and imagine their energy entering your Energetic Intuitive Body. Their energy is now available for you to work with.

For example, if you feel anxious and that your energy is scattered, you can call on the energy of a Smokey Quartz crystal. Once connected, simply use your awareness and/or your breath to move its energy to where you feel you need it in your body. You can also do this to practice Energetic Self-Sovereignty. Simply call on the energy of the crystal or plant you want, and use its energy to clear your energetic intuitive body.

What's on my altar?
Take an inventory of the spiritual tools you use to help you connect to your intuition, and consider if you might be culturally appropriating any of these practices. If you're brand new to this work, you get to start from scratch and build an intuitive toolbox that is relevant and specific to you and your lineage. If you have a more established practice, this may be a moment to make some changes.

Research the practices you currently use, and ask yourself:

What's on your altar?
What spiritual tools do you use?
Where did they come from?
What is their history?
Who do they belong to?
Are they part of my ancestry?
Who benefits from you purchasing and using them?

Now consider what you learned about your lineage when you looked at your Ancestor Story in the last chapter. Ask:

What are the practices and tools of my lineage?
How can I learn more about them?

How could I bring these tools into my practice?

Who am I "following"?

Look at who you follow on social media and notice if you're only consuming content from teachers of the same background, gender, abilities, race, or ethnicity as you. Are you listening and learning from Black, Indigenous, People of Color (BIPOC)? Are you learning from the LGBTQIA+ community? What do they have to say about intuition and spirituality? What do they have to share about the injustices and imbalances we face as a collective?

This is how you begin to dismantle the spiritual echo chamber, and it means listening and learning from other people's truths so you can discover more about your own. By discovering what others are facing in the world we live in, we can work on creating change that benefits everyone.

As a rule of engagement, and a way to build relationship authentically with communities who have historically been oppressed, do your own research about any subjects or issues that come that you don't fully understand. Asking for free advice or guidance in a person's DMs or comments is another form of exploitation. Listen, notice what comes up for you, and look back through their old posts and other online resources to learn more. If you want to connect with them further, pay them for their offerings, knowledge and services.

⬦⬦⬦⬦⬦

GUIDED MEDITATION

The guided meditation for this chapter is called "Meditation for Conscious Intuition." It will help you to lean in to those uncomfortable feelings as you learn how to be with your whole self. You can find it in the online portal.

REPEAT TO INVOKE CONSCIOUS INTUITION

I connect with authenticity

I connect with integrity

I connect with honor

I am the shadow and the light

I am a sacred intuitive vessel

I am part of the collective energy

I embody my values

I go deeper to know myself and my practice

I question what my truth is

I am in my intuitive power

I am in my truth

I am a Conscious Intuitive

11

INTUITION AND THE COLLECTIVE

You're here. You made it. You have remembered that *you are intuitive*. One of the reasons you picked up this book was because you were craving a deeper connection to yourself and the world around you. What I hope you've learned is that your intuition is here to help you with this by guiding you to be in your truth, as you walk your healing journey, and stand in your Energetic Self-Sovereignty.

Our journey together has also shown you how the unique energetic imprint that is YOU is part of the wider collective energy of our planet. That how you show up in the world, every thought and action that you take, has an impact on the whole of humanity. This is an especially important message for the times we are moving through together as we progress though the 21st century—a moment in our history when it is imperative that we reclaim this natural born gift and ancient human technology.

The same way a personal Spiritual Reactivation asks an individual to stand fully in their truth, as the masks fall away and we are asked to confront uncomfortable truths as fantasy and delusion fall away, our planet is currently undergoing its own process of Reactivation. We stand together at the crossroads of change, as all the shadows, the hidden truths, the trauma and the collective wounding of the planet and her people rise to the surface. There is no more hiding from this, as the entire human race embarks on a deep journey into the underworld of our collective energetic system.

You only have to turn on the news to get a taste of how unsettling this mass reactivation process is. As if the alarm has gone off, and every cell in our beings is vibrating with the shockwaves of the new. But what we are being presented with is an opportunity to transform, and to disrupt and dismantle systems that are running out of time.

It is a time of revolution, when egoic values and corrupted systems built on colonialism, patriarchy, and control will crumble and fall. For as each of us wakes up to our individual spiritual truth, we are beginning to see that these systems can only exist as long as we are complicit with them. That while we blame society, we forget that we *are* society. And that radical, lasting change, can only begin as each and every one of us chooses to enact this in our lives.

As the foundations on which our civilization has been built begin to rattle and shake, it's natural to feel ungrounded, fearful, and as if the world is literally "ending." But what looks like chaos, is all part of the evolutionary process that our souls signed up for when we incarnated during these times. And the same way the natural world evolves over millennia, the evolutionary shift that we are experiencing isn't going to happen overnight.

We are deep in the throes of a lengthy process that could last our entire lifetimes. But rather than feel overwhelmed by this, *we can take comfort in what we intuitively know to be true*: that ultimately, everything that is unfolding is for the greater good, as the power structure of the planet is reorganized to bring more freedom, equity, and unity to our world.

Your role as an intuitive (remember, this means you and every other person on this planet!) is to become so rooted in your own, unassailable truth, that you are able to hold steady as the world we've known comes unglued. Now that you have access to your gifts, you will be able to use them to guide you during this time, as you practice discernment, take council in your own wisdom over the noise of the world around you, and use your energy as a force for positive change. Never has it been more vital that you are able to trust your truth and take back your power, and be an example to others to do the same.

By living authentically, by simply being YOU, free of the fear-based conditioning that we have been programmed with, your life will send ripples out into the collective that will in turn help usher in the new.

YOU ARE MORE POWERFUL THAN YOU KNOW

So many of the struggles and the traumas and the conflicts that have defined human history have come down to power. Who wants the power, who has the power, who wields the power, and who is abusing the power. Part of what has caused this current collective Reactivation is that the power balance on the planet is all out of whack. The thing is, nobody wants to relinquish power when they have it. Power feels GOOD. And on one level, it makes sense that the people, institutions, and systems that have been hoarding the power are going to try to hold onto it by whatever means necessary. They will fight and do whatever it takes to maintain the status quo.

Essentially, they want to maintain the illusion that they are in control (versus us *all* having a say in how the world turns on her axis). And not just the *people* who currently wield power, but the systems of authority themselves. For example, our governments and political structures have their own power energy. As do the military and policing systems used to maintain law and order, and the banking systems that control the movement and value of wealth. Our education systems, which control what "knowledge" is passed on to the next generation, have the power to influence the beliefs of our descendents. Our healthcare systems, which control who receives medical care, what drugs are available, and how we even perceive "healing," have power over our bodies and our minds. Our technology systems, which control how we work and connect with one another, have the power to shape industry. The system that controls the global supply of food, has the power to control nutritional wellbeing. As you can see, every part of our lives relies on one of these systems of power. And right now, it is as if the entire machine is stalled and on the brink of breaking down, creating an opportunity for a mass redistribution of *power*.

But part of what is "broken" about the current structure, is that it works in favor of some, while robbing others of their power in order to function. It was purposefully built this way to maintain the current power dynamic. Part of our individual awakening is to examine and interrogate how we are privileged (or not) within each of these systems, especially for anybody who identifies as white. Looking at how white privilege extracts and exploits the innate power of those who identify as Black, indigenous, and people of color, and who have endured hundreds of years of oppression based on the color of their skin, and their proximity to indigeneity based on specious classification systems, is part of this evolutionary process.

These systems have also created bias based on gender, with the masculine principle having been exalted, with the feminine being seen as "weaker" and placed in the supporting role—whether this applies to actual human beings who identify as either masculine or feminine, or "masculine" traits, such as productivity and dominance being seen as powerful, while more "feminine" traits, such as caretaking and emotional intelligence, are seen as soft and exploitable. Much of what we have seen in the realm of the #metoo movement and trans rights, for example, can be read as part of the undoing of this gender power structure—as we strive to create equity between the masculine and feminine, so that they can work in harmony within each of us.

So what has all this got to do with intuition? As we've seen, being in your intuitive power is the ultimate way to live in your own authenticity and truth—and you taking back this power is a way of divesting from the existing power structure. The same way that if everybody took their money out of their bank at the same time, the entire banking system would collapse, each of us putting our energy into the current systems that govern us, is what allows them to keep going.

Notice any fear that arises as you read this. Perhaps picturing the collapse of the banking system brings up images of mass panic—as we see each time the stock market takes a dive. This is a normal reaction when faced with the possibility of systemic change ... as there *will* be a period of chaos before a new world order emerges. Any resistance to this part of the evolutionary process is coming from the Ego / Fear Voice.

To counter this, now take a moment to tune in to your Intuitive Voice. What does it have to tell you about this collective evolution? Does it show you that despite the exterior turmoil this is happening as part of a bigger global transformation? How does it make you feel? It might not make sense right now but in your energetic intuitive body is there a knowing that this has to happen?

Each of us being in our intuitive power is vital as we evolve as a collective. This is how we claim full agency and autonomy over our own energy, so that each action we take is another brick in the wall of the new paradigm that is on its way. Only when we are fully in control of our thoughts, our behaviours, our emotions, and our connection to ∞, are we able to live our lives as a force for positive change. When we are connected to our power, and being guided by our intuitive gifts, we are able to trust that whatever difficulties we may find ourselves facing as a result of this mass distribution of power, we are in fact paving a radical path to a better way of living for all. Yes, part of this journey will entail confusion, loss, and feelings of intense discomfort. Any new beginning must be preceded by the destruction of what came before. But our intuition tells us that not only is this okay, we are better equipped to rise to whatever challenges are in store than we know. We are in fact far more powerful than we have been led to believe.

STAY IN YOUR POWER

As old systems cling more desperately to their power in an attempt to maintain control of the collective energy, situations and beliefs that deliberately try to take us out of our power are intensified. These energy "power games" can make us feel anxious, destabilized, uncertain, and fearful. This is a deliberate tactic to take us out of our Energetic Self-Sovereignty, so that our ability to take aligned action is disabled. Some ways this impacts us are through our interactions with social media, the news cycle, and mainstream movies and TV shows. This is why the tools and practices for Energetic Self-Sovereignty shared throughout this book are so important—the irony being that when our energy is scattered it's easy to forget to use them.

You can also use the prompts below to help you when you feel like something has left you energetically drained. When you begin to feel anxious, ungrounded, confused or fearful, pause wherever you are. Take a couple of moments, to ask yourself why you may be feeling this way. Ask:

- Where have I been directing my power and energy recently?
- Have I just had a conversation with someone that has made me feel this way?
- Have I seen or experienced something that has made me feel out of my power?
- What have I just read in the news or on social media?
- Has my Ego / Fear Voice gone into overdrive?
- Have I taken on beliefs, opinions or emotions that aren't aligned with my truth?
- Am I being influenced or pressured by my family or friends, or the community or country I live in?

If you're still uncertain as to why you're feeling out of your power you can also do the Is This My Energy? body scan on page 48 to identify and clear your energetic intuitive body.

Once you have identified what has made you step out of your power, you can release whatever it is to help you feel more anchored, calm and collected by taking a few long, deep breaths into your belly. Then say out loud or in your head, *"I release the energy that is taking me out of my power. YOU HAVE NO POWER OVER ME."* Call on your Spirit Team and ask for shielding to support you to stay in your power.

YOUR TRUTH AND THE COLLECTIVE

Using your intuition in your everyday life will help you stay connected to your own inner truth, but it is also a tool to help you tune in to the collective truth. In an era of misinformation, propaganda, and "alternative facts," this has never been more important. Ask yourself: why would you trust what the news cycle, social media, and the mainstream media outlets are saying, over your own intuitive knowing?

While factions of the mainstream media do their best to remain unbiased and to base their reporting on fact, the truth is all media outlets (including social media) have an agenda—based on the views and opinions of the people running them, as well as belief systems of the readership they are speaking to. This inevitably leads to its own abuses of power, and, as such, the media is another "system" that is up for review right now. As the chaos of the collective Reactivation intensifies, the quality of information we are taking in is essential. It is also vital that we do our own research, and make sure we are consuming news from multiple sources, so we can get a full picture of what's going on. But even more important is for you to discover your own truth within the turmoil. This means using your intuition to ask questions such as: *What do I believe? What is propaganda and what is truth? What feels right for me?*

We're also in a climate of gaslighting and manipulation, which can make it even harder to connect to our truth, and where societal conditioning has made it uncomfortable for us to speak our beliefs and demand our needs be met out of fear of judgment from others. *But the reality is that everyone has their own version of the truth*—which can lead to tension and "in-fighting" as people try to defend their unique point of view. But this is not about "us and them" or "right and wrong" or "good and evil." This is actually another part of the democratization of power, and in the transition it is going to get messy! The key is for you to feel confident about listening to *your* truth within the cacophony of voices that are trying to get your attention—until, ultimately, the power has been redistributed, the noise dies down, and we are able to listen and learn from each other. If you are a person of privilege, it is even more important to "check yourself" for any places you may unconsciously be abusing *your* power.

You might be someone who struggles to express your truth. We've all been programmed to a degree not to share our beliefs, our thoughts, and our emotions—but connecting to your intuition will also help you develop more confidence in this area. The more you connect to your truth, the more freely you will feel called to express it, even if this may look different for everyone. It could be through writing, drawing, painting, organizing community events, donating, protesting, educating others, or however you feel called to share the truth of who you are. But it is vital for you to notice if you are staying silent out of fear of judgment from others. Any time you stay "quiet" you are allowing your power to continue to be manipulated by the systems we are tasked with dismantling.

Using your intuitive gifts to discover how to use your voice and express your truth is paramount. How you decide to use your voice when you get that "Hell Yes" is part of the action and how we divest our energy from the existing power structure. Remember that judgment and fear of what others think of you as an intuitive was one of the main blocks to accessing our intuitive power. The flawed systems and structures will try to gaslight you into not speaking your truth to continue this cycle of fear of using our voices. They don't want you to be fully in your intuitive power and they don't want you to remember that your voice creates change. This is another reason why working with your intuition is a vital piece in our collective evolution.

ALIGN WITH THE POWER OF NATURE

As a result of an imbalance of power in our relationship with Mother Nature, we are also experiencing the tremors of an environmental systems collapse. The ecosystem of our planet relies on each insect, animal, plant, tree, mountain, ocean, and atom of the atmosphere working in harmony, and as humans we are also part of this system. Which means how we own and direct our power is also part of bringing our ecosystem back into balance.

As we are seeing however, this "rebalancing" process is already happening, whether we choose to step up as proactive participants or not. Our Earth is showing us all the ways we have abused, extracted, and plundered her resources, co-opting her energy and her power to maintain the systems of control on the planet. It is increasingly evident that this cannot continue. That she will not *allow* it to.

What is required is a return to the Indigenous and ancestral knowledge of the land, so that the Earth's natural rhythms can be restored. Land and water rights must also be given back to the people they have been stolen from. Given the extent of the damage that has been done, it can be hard to envision how to move forward from here, let alone our individual roles in this. Use the below research exercise as a starting point:

- Start to research who owns the land you live, work and play on. Look for books on local history and folklore. *Native-land.ca* is a resource you can use to help with this.
- Follow and listen to Indigenous leaders in your community and globally, and learn from what they have to say.
- Read about the history of oppression of the Indigenous people who originally inhabited the land you live on.
- Get curious about the local plants and wildlife that grow or live in your area, and how they can be protected.
- Look into the farming techniques that we currently use globally that are from our colonial past.
- Look at the labels of your food to see how far it has travelled to get to your supermarket. How can you buy more local produce? Is there a city farm or local farmers market?
- Learn about sustainable foraging, wildcrafting and land management.
- Research about soil sovereignty and food sovereignty.
- Research about water rights in your country and globally.

It can feel overwhelming to be present with the systemic environmental destruction our planet faces. But becoming educated is the first step to becoming part of the change.

TAKING ACTION IN THE COLLECTIVE

Change can be exhausting and overwhelming. It can feel so much *easier* to slip into the well-worn grooves of what has gone before, even if it wasn't serving us. Faced with the unknown, and unsure what a "different" future may have in store, we may even find ourselves hankering for old ways of doing things, or clinging to the way things used to be. Observing what has gone before, it may even seem like real change isn't possible, so what's the point of trying? It might feel tempting to stick your head in the sand and pretend none of this is happening. But this isn't the time for that.

This is a time to choose hope over despair; possibility over fear. It's a time when we can either choose to be in denial or look at the truth. It's also a time, beyond simply believing in the potential for change, to take action to move the needle forward. Of course you may be feeling disillusioned thinking that no real change will ever happen as it's never happened before. That everything will lose momentum and we'll go back to "normal." But what's different now, is we're being faced with so much *all at once*, there is no option but to change. We can no longer pretend it's not happening, or avoid playing our part. Just like a personal Spiritual Reactivation forces us to look at our shadow and make changes in our lives, we are undergoing a collective Reactivation that is asking us to do the same. Taking aligned, intuitive action, together, is the only way forward, and that is why you are here.

To learn, to grow, and to live in authentic truth with yourself and the collective, means also being a torchbearer for positive change. No matter how uncomfortable or challenging it may seem at first, when you choose to take action from a place of truth you also become an example for others to do the same. In your family, your friendships, your career, your partnerships, and your wider community, it is imperative to "walk the talk" and put your intuition into action.

It's one thing to intuitively know what to do but it's a whole other thing to actually action it. Are you willing to take the risk when your intuition is telling you: "THIS ISN'T RIGHT?" Are you prepared to take back your power, own your truth, and use your voice? This may mean putting your intuition into action to speak out about your sexual trauma, to start an uncomfortable conversation about racism, or to oppose a government bill being used to oppress people's freedoms. Will you stand up and take action for what you believe in when the power structures are acting out to hold onto control?

Here are some suggestions for where to start.

Ask your intuition: What is my next right action?

Your first port of call is to work with ∞ and your Spirit Team for guidance and clarity on what your next action could be. There are a few ways you can do this:

- Call on your Spirit Team in whichever way you have discovered works for you. Ask your Ancestor Guides what action you can take to avoid repeating the mistakes of the past.
- Use the Empty Room exercise to ask your question, and allow yourself to receive guidance through your Intuitive Feeling, Seeing, Hearing, or Knowing.
- Start to notice the themes and patterns that keep recurring in your life in relation to the situation you want to take action on. Go to your Inner Reference Library to discover what they mean for you.
- Use the "Hell Yes, Heck No" technique to get confirmation on the aligned action.
- Work with your dreams and ask for intuitive messages about your next action to appear in dream state.

Remember, the action being asked of you may require you to get uncomfortable. Lean into this, and keep asking for more guidance every step of the way. Any time you feel intuitively called to check in with ∞ and your Spirit Team, you can ask again for the next right action to take.

Check your energy

Our energy levels are all being impacted during this collective Reactivation. Some days you may feel like you have lots of energy and other days you will feel exhausted—making it harder to take action. Tune into your energetic intuitive body and replenish your reserves using the Energetic Self-Sovereignty meditation in Chapter 3 and/or the Grounding Force Field Visualization. It's also vital that you give yourself permission to rest and recharge. You can use your intuition to ask when this is really necessary, and when you may be using feeling tired as an excuse not to take action that feels scary or uncomfortable.

Take action in the present moment

Aligned action requires integrity—and this begins with you doing what you can to heal the present moment. It means being able to take an honest look at what's happening in your life and how the way you have been living is impacting the collective. Which again, is not always comfortable or easy. Here are some questions you can use to check in with where you're at:

Where am I not being honest with myself?
Where am I in denial?
Where am I resisting transformation?
What am I afraid of?
What scares me about taking back my power?
Where am I curious about what's happening in the collective?
What does freedom look like for me?
What does freedom look like for the collective?

Journal your responses in your Intuition Journal to help you get clear.

Envision the change you want to see

When things are in flux and the path ahead isn't clear, it can be easy to lose sight of how we want our lives to be. All we can see is the confusion of the present moment, making us doubt that a new vision for the future is even possible. The below Envisioning practice will help you gain clarity on where we are going—in our individual lives, and as a collective. Check yourself for any spiritual bypassing (for example, pretending that any wounding or trauma that led to the current situation didn't happen or wasn't "our fault")—and come to the exercise from a frequency of love, hope, and integrity. This exercise always begins with you, and then moves out into your community, and into the collective.

Either by closing your eyes and using your Imagination or by writing in a journal, begin by asking:

What does my life feel like in the future? (the emotions you want to experience)
What does my life look like in the future? (the actions you want to be taking)

What does my community feel like in the future?

What does my community look like in the future?

What does the collective feel like in the future?
What does the collective look like in the future?

Write down in your journal what comes up for you. You can then go back to them as an anchor point or "safe space" to return to in any uncertainty you might face. Your future visions might also inspire you to take action in the present moment.

This is different from asking your intuition about future possibilities, as it allows you to "feel into" a new vision for the future in the present moment. Then, any time you are experiencing anxiety, fear, panic or uncertainty, you can come back to your vision for the future in an instant. Of course, this may change, but when approached with integrity this exercise will help you tap into a vision for the future that's rooted in your truth, your wisdom, and your power.

◇◇◇◇◇

Your intuition is your guiding light—and ultimately, being a conscious intuitive means it is your job to shine this light into the shadows of your life, and into the core wounding and traumas that are impacting the collective. This is *all* of our responsibility as we evolve and heal together, and our intuition is what will help us see into the unseen. As much as your intuition is a tool to help you live as your most authentic self and to live the life you are here to live, being a conscious intuitive means also recognizing that everything is connected. That it is impossible for one of us to live our "best life" until *all of us* are able to enjoy the same privileges and freedoms as us.

As we complete our work here together, I invite you once again to notice and pay attention to all that is unfolding for you during this universal Reactivation. I want you to remember that you always have access to ∞ and that you are being supported by your Spirit Team every step of the way, as you begin to embody the energy of grace, courage, authenticity and inner strength. I want you to know, more than anything, that your intuition is here to guide you through these challenging and uncertain times, and that it is your portal to standing firm and unshakable in your Energetic Self-Sovereignty.

Please do not underestimate the impact of this. It is only when each and every individual is able to walk in our sovereignty that we will see a true redistribution of power. This is when we will begin to see political sovereignty, as well as to know personal sovereignty over information, and of our bodies, our health, our food, the environment, and even the cosmos. This is when we will begin to understand that each thought, word, and action that we make, is bringing its own energy to our fellow humans, to the natural world, and to all that is.

You were born at this time on this planet for a reason. Your soul chose to be here so that you could be part of the change. It is time to trust your truth, take back your power, and remember that you are intuitive.

GUIDED MEDITATION

The guided meditation for this chapter is to help you with "Envisioning a Positive Future" for your life and for the collective. Use it as an anchor to ground you during these challenging yet transformational times. You can find it in the online portal.

REPEAT TO INVOKE UNITY AND COLLECTIVE CHANGE

I am intuitive

I am in my power and in my truth

I am in my Energetic Self-Sovereignty

My energy is part of the collective

My energy is part of the reactivation

My energy is part of evolution

I am transforming

I am taking action

I am the change

I am united with others and my actions

I am connected to Mother Earth and nature

I release the old and step into the new

I act with unity, authenticity and courage

I act to create freedom and equality

I act with ∞ and my Spirit Team at my side

I am hope

I am love

I am intuitive

GLOSSARY

Ancestor Story: My term for the web of themes, patterns, blocks, and beliefs we have inherited from our ancestors—both our ancestry going back hundreds of years, and also our immediate lineage: parents, grandparents, and great-grandparents

Astral Travel: The experience of consciously leaving your energetic intuitive body while sleeping or in meditation to travel to different places through time and space.

Chakra: Chakras are energy points located all over the body. These energy points are portals to receive information from ∞ and reactivate a connection in your energetic intuitive body.

Collective: The collective is a term to describe the energy of our planet and our individual connection to it. Every human, animal and plant is part of the collective.

Conscious Intuitive: A Conscious Intuitive is someone who connects to their intuitive gifts with the awareness that each action creates a ripple effect, and that the more aligned we are with our inner guidance, the more we can have a positive impact in the world.

Creative Imagination: Our individual connection to universal creative energy, and a key component of our energetic intuitive body.

Crown: The crown or crown chakra, located at the top of the head, is one way of receiving the flow of energy between ∞ and your energetic intuitive body.

Déjà Vu: A moment in which we experience something as if it has happened before. Déjà vu can also be an intuitive marker, or visual sign, that you're on the right path.

Ego / Fear Voice: Your Ego is the voice of your external identity, or how you see yourself in the world. Our Fear Voice is the voice of our inner survival instinct. Combined, they create the Ego / Fear Voice, which kicks in with well-meaning "advice" during times of panic and acute stress and discomfort.

Empath: A term to describe people who are more energetically sensitive and who have the ability to feel other people's feelings.

Energy: Everything in the world is made up of energy. The seen and the unseen. Our bodies, our homes, our emotions, and the connection between people, nature, our built structures, and our intuition. It's all energy.

Energetic Forcefield: A way to shield and protect your own energy field as you practice Energetic Self-Sovereignty.

Energetic Intuitive Body: You. Yes, you. Your whole body is intuitive. Every single cell, neuron, nerve ending, and ampule of energy.

Energetic Self-Sovereignty: The state and practice of residing in your own energy field, and of removing or blocking energy from others from your energetic intuitive body.

Inner Reference Library: A bank of images, sounds, and other sensory impressions that have been logged in our memory and infused with "meaning." Can be used to decipher intuitive messages.

Instant Hit: When we receive intuitive guidance and instantly know exactly what it means and what action to take.

Intuitive Gifts: The unique way that you, and you alone, receive your intuitive guidance.

Intuitive Heart: Your heart is a specific portal in the intuitive body where your intuitive power lies, and the place where love meets intuition. A powerful combination.

Intuitive Portal: The energetic gateways and pathways to your intuitive gifts.

Intuitive Power: Your ability to own and trust your inner guidance, enabling you to live your authentic truth and express your creative imagination.

Intuitive Voice: The voice of your inner guidance and of the energetic intuitive body.

Intuition Journal: A place to record the intuitive messages you receive and take notes to help you learn how to work with your unique intuitive gifts.

Invocation: Words to be spoken out loud to connect with ∞ and to "call in" the intention of the invocation.

Lucid Dreaming: State in which you are able to control the dream narrative while asleep. If you are a lucid dreamer then this is part of your intuitive gifts, as you can ask for guidance within your dream state.

Message: A piece of intuitive guidance.

New Age: Movement of the 1960s and 1970s referring to the dawning of the astrological Age of Aquarius, which it was believed would catapult us into a "New Age" of personal transformation and healing.

Now Age: Phrase describing the evolution of the New Age movement to reflect life in the 21st Century.

Other Side: The world of ∞ that exists beyond our human world.

Power: The part of our life force energy that gives us agency to act on our free will and live as our true selves.

Past Life: A life you experienced before your soul reincarnated into this body and this lifetime.

Shadow Self: The parts of our personality we might see as negative or weak and that we hide away. This may be our anger, our jealousy, our desire, our fear, or our feelings of being unlovable or "not enough." We all have a shadow self, even if we see ourselves as happy or a "good person."

Spirit Team: Team of "helpers" made up of Spirit Guides, ancestors and deceased loved ones who are here to help guide you, protect you and send you messages from the other side.

Spiritual Bypassing: Using our relationship to the "spiritual" as a way to avoid facing the potentially painful, challenging, or inconvenient truths in ourselves and in the world we live in.

Spiritual Labeling: Human labels used to describe all things ∞.

Spiritual Reactivation: A time in life when events herald a return to our inner power, a deeper connection to the meaning of our life, and our relationship to who we are in the world.

Starseeds: Advanced beings from a different planet, star, or galaxy.

Third Eye: The third eye chakra or pineal gland has traditionally been associated with "seeing gifts." It is located between your eyebrows.

∞

ACKNOWLEDGEMENTS

Firstly, thanks to my parents, family and friends who have supported me through the writing of this book. I never felt "alone" writing these words during a global pandemic. Although you couldn't support me in person, your FaceTime calls, messages and voice notes from all across the globe were an important source of encouragement. Who would have thought that one of my favorite places to write during this time would be in bed! (I thought authors wrote their books at a fancy desk....lol...maybe they do?)

Thank you to all the teachers, mentors and guides that have contributed to my personal growth and transformation. For asking the right questions of me and encouraging me to be my authentic self.

Laura, Mum, thanks for taking me to "diddleydop" all those years ago. Who would have thought it would have ended up here? Rae, one of the most dialled in, keeping it on the down-low intuitives I know. Loving all our yawning video chats (hello Spirit) and silly face pulls.

Ruby, for the intuitive editing and being so "in tune" with the manuscript. It was a dream process bringing all the ideas together, and it felt like we just "knew" what this book wanted to be. The conversation when we both shared that X did not want to be called "Spirit" is one I'll always remember. It's an honour to be the first author for Numinous Books.

And to the rest of the team for the support when I get the intuitive "HELL YES" to create, and for making things happen with quick turnaround deadlines and multiple moving parts. Thanks for being part of this intuitive mission.

Thank you to the community of intuitives who have supported me over the years in one-to-one sessions, events, workshops, and to the listeners of the podcast, "So You Think You're Intuitive." Your questions and musings about your own gifts have inspired many parts of this book.

Thank you to the racial and social justice educators who I'm continually learning from to unpack my own racism and unconscious biases. Thank you for sharing your wisdom, experiences and leading the way to create change during this pivotal time on the planet: Rachel Ricketts, Layla F. Saad, Dr. Jennifer Mullan, Seeding Sovereignty, Leesa Renee Hall, Tricia Hersey of The Nap Ministry, and Allen Salway.

And thank you to my Spirit Team for always guiding me. Even when it felt like I was alone. I understand that it was all for a reason. Thanks for reminding me to get out of my own way, to trust the plan, and for reminding me to be in the flow of life. Running to stand still.

∞∞∞

This book was written on the traditional, ancestral and unceded traditional territories of the Coast Salish peoples – xʷməθkʷəy̓əm (Musqueam), sḵwx̱wú7mesh (Squamish), and selíĺwitulh (Tsleil-Waututh) nations.

I am a guest and visitor here.

CONTINUE THE YOU ARE INTUITIVE CONVERSATION

My greatest desire is that this book has helped you trust your truth, take back your power and reactivate your intuitive gifts. There has never been a more important time for this. If you'd like to continue learning about and continue deepening your intuitive gifts, you can:

Join the INTUITIVE Community. You don't need to feel alone with your gifts. Join my online community and connect with others dedicated to reactivating and using their intuitive gifts at www.youareintuitive.com. Plus, you'll receive access to on demand workshops, live events, private groups, guest teachers from around the world, and intuitive conversations with others. Includes access to the free guided meditations, set to binaural beats, that are highlighted in each chapter of the book.

Subscribe to the *So You Think You're Intuitive* podcast. A straight-talking podcast, created to help you reactivate, grow and trust your intuition so you can live a more empowered, abundant and connected life.

Sign up for the Newsletter. Receive inspired event information, announcements, and practical tips on how you can work with your intuition in your everyday life straight to your inbox.

Share with #IAmIntuitive and #IntuitiveHits. Join me in using these hashtags to highlight insights, breakthroughs and intuitive hits across social media.

For more information and to join the community visit:
www.youareintuitive.com
www.natalie-miles.com
Instagram: @iamnataliemiles

Natalie Miles is an international psychic medium, writer, speaker, and host of top spiritual podcast *"So You Think You're Intuitive?"* Known for her down-to-earth approach, it is her mission to make intuition accessible to everyone. In her work with individuals and groups, she guides clients to use their intuition to look at what's holding them back in the here and now, empowering them to take action on their inner truths. She lives in Vancouver, Canada. *www.nataliemiles.com*

CPSIA information can be obtained
at www.ICGtesting.com
Printed in the USA
LVHW041205210920
666653LV00001B/1